The Collected Shorter Poems

of Kenneth Rexroth

BOOKS BY KENNETH REXROTH

POEMS

The Collected Shorter Poems
The Collected Longer Poems
Flower Wreath Hill: Later Poems
The Selected Poems

PLAYS

Beyond the Mountains

CRITICISM & ESSAYS

The Classics Revisited
More Classics Revisited

TRANSLATIONS

100 Poems from the Chinese
100 More Poems from the Chinese: Love and the Turning Year
100 Poems from the Japanese
100 More Poems from the Japanese
Seasons of Sacred Lust: The Selected Poems of Kazuko Shiraishi
    (*with Ikuko Atsumi, John Solt, Carol Tinker, and
    Yasuyo Morita*)
Selected Poems of Pierre Reverdy
Li Ch'ing-chao: Complete Poems (*with Ling Chung*)
Women Poets of China (*with Ling Chung*)
Women Poets of Japan (*with Ikuko Atsumi*)

AUTOBIOGRAPHY

An Autobiographical Novel

Kenneth Rexroth

The Collected Shorter Poems

New Directions

Certain of these poems appeared originally in *Accent, American Stuff, Angry Penguins, Approach, The Ark, Atlantic Monthly, Blues, Briarcliff Quarterly, Coastlines, Compass, Contour, Cronos, Diogenes, Direction, Epoch, Factotum, Fantasy, Furioso, Goad, The Golden Goose, Horizon, Illiterati, Meanjin Papers, Midwest, Modern Verse, Morada, Nativity, The Needle, New Directions, New Masses, New Mexico Quarterly Review, The New Republic, Now, Objectivist Anthology, Outposts, Pacific, Pacific Spectator, Pagany, Partisan Review, Poetry, Poetry Australia, Poetry Folios, Poetry Quarterly, The Quarterly Review of Literature, Resistance, Retort, The Tiger's Eye, The Windsor Quarterly, Little Anthology of World Poetry* (copyright 1952 by Charles Scribner's Sons), *New World Writing* (copyright 1954 by The New American Library of World Literature), *Perspectives, U.S.A.* (copyright 1952, 1955 by Intercultural Publications, Inc.,) *Poetry in Crystal* (copyright © 1962 Steuben Glass).

The poem "A Lemma by Constance Reid" is based on material appearing in *From Zero to Infinity: What Makes Numbers Interesting*, Copyright © 1955, 1960 by the author, Constance Reid. Thomas Y. Crowell Company, New York, publishers.

Library of Congress catalog card number: 66-17818

ISBN 0-8112-0367-0

ISBN 0-8112-0178-3 (pbk)

Manufactured in the United States of America.
Published simultaneously in Canada by Penguin Books Canada Limited

New Directions Books are published for James Laughlin by New Directions Publishing Corporation.
80 Eighth Avenue, New York 10011

NINTH PRINTING

GÖDEL'S PROOF

NEW POEMS 1965

"A *self-contained system is a contradiction of terms.* QED"

For my daughters
Mary and Katharine
and for Carol, these new poems.

When the nightingale cries
All night and all day,
I have my sweetheart
Under the flower
Till the watch from the tower
Cries, "Lovers, rise!
The dawn comes and the bright day."

ANONYMOUS PROVENÇAL

ANDROMEDA CHAINED TO HER ROCK
THE GREAT NEBULA IN HER HEART

I

The ache
The heart is never well
The incurable pain
The iron warp of time
The shrinking web of life
The grey unquiet ocean
Under uninhabited fog
The roar which always begins
And is never still
Which nothing will ever stop
In the grey
In the white
In the bitter throat
Against the concave wall
The little pile of soiled bones
Nails will never glitter
Brain will never ooze
Gulf will no longer open
O heart
O charred heart
O broken eye

II

Anguish and form and prayer
No excuse no betrayal
No dimension in space or time
Without caution without consequence without motion
The many blades of the revolving razors
The many tears of the breaking sorrow
The fear of the bear the ghost of the bear
The gear of care that is always here
When the cross of words spells zero
There are trees in the sea
There are red columns on the horizon
And fear everywhere
And every year no word at all for all her pain

And she said I want just what you want she said
Just a big box full of old veils
And the shears were always cutting at night
Always far away or always near cutting
Move the cube at right angles to everywhere
At right angles to itself
Lips to lips and eyes to eyes move
At right angles
Hands on hands edges
Spin in light beams
In the rattleflake of brightness
Gone
Call
Kindred
Keep
Coinage

III

O fire around fire in fire of fire with fire
By fire alone
Fire pointed fire the star in star
And the self falls in god shimmer
The visionary shipwreck
The kidnapped ecstasy
The copulation of the lightning and the lighthouse
A skirt lifts its tent of perfume
A woman's frail veiled sight moved stirred
Stirred the virgin in the womb of the man
Ishtar the tree of fiery stars
The eye wraps itself up in its retina
The old dark transmigrating eye
A boat of oak sails
Under a tree of silver
Under a crown of thorns
Gold spring blue autumn purple winter
Song alone
Or the harp in a crystal room
Snow falling ever more heavily
The room growing steadily darker
Bones like white wires cry out in their dream

4

IV

Eyes in moss
Salt in mouth
Stone in heart
An owl rings the changes of silence
Torn head
Crow's wings
Black eyeballs
Poison seeps through the parabolic sand
The rock on fire
Ice falls towards the sun
The hurled axe
Lost in the future
Of an automatic and anonymous dream
The brazen serpent
In the desert of hallucination
Manna is the excrement of vermin
What is the shadow
Crawling on the eggshell
What chorale
Flees in the sea shell
The bite of the gods
In the wilderness
Metamorphosing the demigods
Thunder lost in shadow
The arc with its unknown spectrum
Of colors never seen before
Infants falling
In the web of sudden geometries
And caution awry
In the power of these hearts
O tower in the dark
Chord in perfume
Day of wrath
Morning of delusion
The iron crow wings
Bear away the torn head
Into the fragile sky
Into the rapture of the depths
Where the blood runs cold

TRAVELERS IN EREWHON

You open your
Dress on the dusty
Bed where no one
Has slept for years
An owl moans on the roof
You say
My dear my
Dear
In the smoky light of the old
Oil lamp your shoulders
Belly breasts buttocks
Are all like peach blossoms
Huge stars far away far apart
Outside the cracked window pane
Immense immortal animals
Each one only an eye
Watch
You open your body
No end to the night
No end to the forest
House abandoned for a lifetime
In the forest in the night
No one will ever come
To the house
Alone
In the black world
In the country of eyes

OAXACA 1925

You were a beautiful child
With troubled face, green eyelids
And black lace stockings
We met in a filthy bar
You said
"My name is Nada
I don't want anything from you
I will not take from you
I will give you nothing"
I took you home down alleys
Splattered with moonlight and garbage and cats
To your desolate disheveled room
Your feet were dirty
The lacquer was chipped on your fingernails
We spent a week hand in hand
Wandering entranced together
Through a sweltering summer
Of guitars and gunfire and tropical leaves
And black shadows in the moonlight
A lifetime ago

GRADUALISM

We slept naked
On top of the covers and woke
In the chilly dawn and crept
Between the warm sheets and made love
In the morning you said
"It snowed last night on the mountain"
High up on the blue black diorite
Faint orange streaks of snow
In the ruddy dawn
I said
"It has been snowing for months
All over Canada and Alaska
And Minnesota and Michigan
Right now wet snow is falling
In the morning streets of Chicago
Bit by bit they are making over the world
Even in Mexico even for us"

OPEN THE BLIND

Nests in the eaves stir in the dawn
Ephemeral as our peace
Morning prayer
Grace before food
I understand
The endless sky the small earth
The shadow cone
Your shining
Lips and eyes
Your thighs drenched with the sea
A telescope full of fireflies
Innumerable nebulae all departing
Ten billion years before we ever met

HIGH PROVENCE

Every evening at seven o'clock
We met under the soaring swallows
In the dense shade of the ancient plane trees
At the same café table
On a little square of golden limestone houses
Dry grass and gravel
Where a fountain spoke softly
The language of the dwellers
In the center of the earth
Rose and green gold and blue
Smoke of olive and wine twigs
From the supper stoves
High up swallows
Laced the immense sky
We kissed in the perfumed evening
And walked off hand in hand
Along a winding road
Over a Roman bridge
Each bucket of the mossy mill wheel
That revolved so slowly
Through the vanishing water
From the dark underground
To the twilit sky
Held an aquarium
Full of brilliant fish
No one had ever seen before
We sat on the hillside and looked back
Over the town and counted the bells
And the new stars
Hazy hair flesh like a plume
Did you watch this half moon
Ten hours ago when it went by
The end of your steep street
Swimming over the Mediterranean

CAMARGUE

Green moon blaze
Over violet dancers
Shadow heads catch fire
Forget forget
Forget awake aware dropping in the well
Where the nightingale sings
In the blooming pomegranate
You beside me
Like a colt swimming slowly in kelp
In the nude sea
Where ten thousand birds
Move like a waved scarf
On the long surge of sleep

AMONG THE CYPRESSES AT THE END OF THE WAY OF THE CROSS

Will you eat water melon
Or drink lemonade
Beside San Miniato
This hot twilight
Arno blurring in its white dry cobbled bed
Wine honey olive oil
Fill the air with their secret vapors
And a black potter
Treads treads treads
Her wheel shaping a pot
With a template cut from your flesh
Lovers whimper in the dusk
We are lost do you hear
We are all lost
As the hundred bells break
And the stars speak

SOTTOPORTICO SAN ZACCARIA

It rains on the roofs
As it rains in my poems
Under the thunder
We fit together like parts
Of a magic puzzle
Twelve winds beat the gulls from the sky
And tear the curtains
And lightning glisters
On your sweating breasts
Your face topples into dark
And the wind sounds like an army
Breaking through dry reeds
We spread our aching bodies in the window
And I can smell the odor of hay
In the female smell of Venice

LEAVING L'ATELIER —
AIX-EN-PROVENCE

Bare trees
Smoky lavender twigs
All the world
Receding horizontal grey blue panels
Ochre walls
Piebald pink tile roofs
Black jagged olive trees killed in the winter of great cold
Everywhere feathers of silver green new olive sprouts
Everywhere red brown plowed fields
Stubs of waiting vines
Hoarfrost on the dark purple plum buds
A black white and green magpie
In wavy flight
Under the morning moon

11

TIME IS AN INCLUSION SERIES
SAID McTAGGART

5 POEMS ON THIS SUBJECT

I

In just a minute we will say goodbye
I will drive away and see you
Cross the boulevard in the rear view mirror
Maybe you will make out the back of my head
Disappearing in the traffic
And then we will never see one another ever again
It will happen in just another minute now

II

Willow Street
Street of bitter leaves
Three generations of whores in the windows
Mother daughter granddaughter
Whose fox are you
Nobody's fox I'm a lone fox
A lone black fox a lone blue fox
Blue fox that's me
The best head on Willow Street
She's dead Helen is dead Dolores is dead
Willow Street is only an embayment
In a ten-story housing project
Willow Street is gone along with
The street of bad boys the street of bad girls
The street where the heart rests
Will they leave even a tiny alley
To name after me

III

Talk in a dark room
Birds fly into the clouded mirror
And never come back
The mirror wears out

IV

For a very long time now
I have been following a black vine
I cannot find the root
I cannot find the tip
There is a high wall of thorns
There is a thick wall of thorns
Around an unknown castle
The thorns are covered with flowers
Each flower is different
But their odor is the perfume
Of a body I have lost

V

Thousands of white scattered
Petals on the waters of hours
Moonlight music surging sea
Commonplace sentiments
Heartbreaks and kisses
Singing voices and voices
Far down the misty beach
By the driftwood fires
Singing forever forever

PHAEDO

After Midnight Mass
In the first black subzero hour of Christmas
I take a twig and white piece of paper
And show you the fragile shadow of Sirius
The Dog Star guarding the Manger
Sleeping at the foot of the Cross

PARK IN THE PUBLIC'S
OR IN THE PUBLIC, PARKS

For Parks Hitchcock's magazine "Kyack"

Cessible
Inack
Cessibleinack
In Nyack
Inacessible the evidence is
They are all intransitive
You can't get Through
You can't get Anyplace
Not with them Zeno knew it
You know Zeno
Zenon Cruel Zenon D'Elée
M. Zenon
Cessible
Inack
On the Isle of Dogs
In the Horse Latitudes
Gentlemen by the Bowels of Christ I regret that I have
    only one fox to feed for my country that is what
    Bishop Latimore said as he was being bit and et
        in the Horse Latitudes
                On the Isle of Dogs
Cessible cessible
In Nyack
N.Y.

Attached to their harpoons by long rawhide cords were in-
flated whole seal skins a couple of seals of air to each
harpoon they came as close as possible and rammed
home the harpoons by main force the whale dove
but the floats of sealskin pulled him back to the
surface again and then they would ram in another
harpoon and finally when he was worn out the leader
would come directly up to his snout and stab him
through the eye into the brain

You wouldn't think Eskimos could do that would you
The whale is comparatively inaccessible to Stone Age Man
And the Eskimos unless they tempt Fate are inaccessible
    to the whale

| In Nyack | Cessible | Not in a |
| N.Y. | Inack | Kyack |

SONG FOR A DANCER

I dream my love goes riding out
Upon a coal black mare.
A cloud of dark all about
Her—her floating hair.

She wears a short green velvet coat.
Her blouse is of red silk,
Open to her swan like throat,
Her breasts white as milk.

Her skirt is of green velvet, too,
And shows her silken thigh,
Purple leather for her shoe,
Dark as her blue eye.

From her saddle grows a rose.
She rides in scented shade.
Silver birds sing as she goes
This song that she made:

"My father was a nightingale,
My mother a mermaid.
Honeyed notes that never fail
Upon my lips they laid."

OTTFFSSENTE

twelve
a dozen
a docent
a hundred does in the zendo
does
1905
down on Victoria Nyazi
The African Princess by Erasmus B. Black
The Lady or the Tiger by Claude Balls
does
dozing sing do
oh do
from dark to full fill filled and fully factual
does
there is at least an entity a
there is at least an entity not a called b
fundamental to the assumption of duality
is the assumption that the class of classes
is itself a class
that's what b is
don't you see
A B C D
goldfish
out of order springs the multifarious world
out of order
oh do
everything going joyfully everywhere
in all the gleaming myriad dimensions of space
do do
oh do
to the mathematically mature it is well known that there
is no such thing as the correct missing number in any
specified sequence. It is possible to insert any number
    whatever
and find a formula which will justify the sequence term for
    term
but the does were missing

from the zendo garden
a dozen does
and the singular literate goldfish
from the crystal deep
said the knowing
docent to the dozen
unknowing
dozing
Africans
who said
oh do
sing
so the Princess
the Lady
Claude
and the Tiger
all sang
do.

CINQUE TERRE

A voice sobs on colored sand
Where colored horses run
Athwart the surf
Us alone in the universe
Where griefs move like the sea
Of the love lost
Under the morning star
Creeping down the sky
Into pale blind water
And we make love
At the very edge of the cliff
Where the vineyards end
In a fringe of ancient
Silver olive trees

TOOK

take it bright day first hour
single chime clear water one thought
nobody has it
take age
take again
take anger
take anguish
point take point
or yellow collars question
take and take
nobody
nobody rode the sheep and has it
take nobody and got away nobody
so bright and salty
so bright and blue
young nobody has it
take girlish
and fans and blades
and glittering scales
take time
and mark it
dogged dogged
but what dogged
makes merry
takes and calves answers
each each
when the bears are polar
it all goes round and round
and rockets and rackets
take time take time
the time nobody ever had
take it all away take it far away
                    and
                    hide

it somewhere under the fine sand filled with shards of pots
 shaped like the torsos of splendor where everything is
 hidden and never will be deciphered and all the camels
 will die before anybody gets there and not one of the
 angels will ever come back
as
took

A FLUTE OVERHEARD

Grey summer
Low tide the sea in the air
A flute song
In a neighboring house
Forty years ago
Socrates on death
The pages turn
The clear voice
Sea fog in the cypress
My daughter calls
From the next room
After forty years
A girl's candid face
Above my desk
Twenty-five years dead
Grey summer fog
And the smell of the living sea
A voice on the moving air
Reading Socrates on death

THE WHEEL REVOLVES

You were a girl of satin and gauze
Now you are my mountain and waterfall companion.
Long ago I read those lines of Po Chu I
Written in his middle age.
Young as I was they touched me.
I never thought in my own middle age
I would have a beautiful young dancer
To wander with me by falling crystal waters,
Among mountains of snow and granite,
Least of all that unlike Po's girl
She would be my very daughter.

The earth turns towards the sun.
Summer comes to the mountains.
Blue grouse drum in the red fir woods
All the bright long days.
You put blue jay and flicker feathers
In your hair.
Two and two violet green swallows
Play over the lake.
The blue birds have come back
To nest on the little island.
The swallows sip water on the wing
And play at love and dodge and swoop
Just like the swallows that swirl
Under and over the Ponte Vecchio.
Light rain crosses the lake
Hissing faintly. After the rain
There are giant puffballs with tortoise shell backs
At the edge of the meadow.
Snows of a thousand winters
Melt in the sun of one summer.
Wild cyclamen bloom by the stream.
Trout veer in the transparent current.
In the evening marmots bark in the rocks.
The Scorpion curls over the glimmering ice field.

A white crowned night sparrow sings as the moon sets.
Thunder growls far off.
Our campfire is a single light
Amongst a hundred peaks and waterfalls.
The manifold voices of falling water
Talk all night.
Wrapped in your down bag
Starlight on your cheeks and eyelids
Your breath comes and goes
In a tiny cloud in the frosty night.
Ten thousand birds sing in the sunrise.
Ten thousand years revolve without change.
All this will never be again.

ORGANIZATION MEN IN AFFLUENT SOCIETY

It is deep twilight, my wife
And girls are fixing supper
In the kitchen. I turn out
The reading lamp and rest my eyes.
Outside the window the snow
Has turned deep blue. *Anthony
and Cleopatra* after a trying day. I think of
Those vigorous rachitic
Men and women taking off
Their clothes of lace and velvet
And gold brocade and climbing
Naked into bed together
Lice in their stinking perfumed
Armpits, the bed full of bugs.

THE HANGED MAN

Storm lifts from Wales
And blows dark over England,
And over my head
As I stand above the Teme,
And look out across Ludlow and the dark castle,
And the ringing church tower.
Clear bells on the storm,
And grey rain on the river,
And me where I will not come again,
And pain I doubt that formal poet ever knew
Who wrote "This is me"
Anent the page of one too cowardly to love.
Ache and hunger fill the lives
Of those who dare not give or take.
Misery is all the lot of the unlovable ones,
And of rejected lovers,
But not one of these knows the empty horror
Of the slow conquering, long fought off,
Realization that love assumed and trusted
Through years of mutual life
Had never been there at all.
The bells of St. Lawrence
Sprinkle their music over the town.
Silver drops, gathered in Bermuda,
Shimmer and are lost in the brown English water.
It is all just like the poet said.

YIN AND YANG

It is spring once more in the Coast Range
Warm, perfumed, under the Easter moon.
The flowers are back in their places.
The birds back in their usual trees.
The winter stars set in the ocean.
The summer stars rise from the mountains.
The air is filled with atoms of quicksilver.
Resurrection envelops the earth.
Geometrical, blazing, deathless,
Animals and men march through heaven,
Pacing their secret ceremony.
The Lion gives the moon to the Virgin.
She stands at the crossroads of heaven,
Holding the full moon in her right hand,
A glittering wheat ear in her left.
The climax of the rite of rebirth
Has ascended from the underworld
Is proclaimed in light from the zenith.
In the underworld the sun swims
Between the fish called Yes and No.

CHINESE POEMS

I

Day after day the rain falls.
Week after week the grass grows.
Year after year the river flows.
Seventy years, seventy years,
The wheel of dreams revolves.

Wang Hung Kung

II

A thousand mountains without a bird.
Ten thousand miles with no trace of man.
A boat. An old man in a straw raincoat,
Alone in the snow, fishing in the freezing river.

Liu Tsung-yuan

III

I will always remember you
Entering the gate of childhood in the season
When plum blossoms give way to cherry blossoms.

Wang Hung Kung

THE ART OF WORLDLY WISDOM
(1920 - 1930)

This little book, dear Andrée,
is all the memorial of our
great love. I miss you always.
And I hope that you, when
you drank from the waters
of death with the new dead,
drank no forgetfulness of me.

ANONYMOUS

IN THE MEMORY OF
ANDREE REXROTH

a

is a question of mutual being
a question of congruence or
proximity a question of
a sudden passage in air beyond
a window a long controlled fall
of music or is congruence
an infusion illumination have
you waited at places have
you seen places have
you said where have
you said adverbs now
air goes up and in glitter
out of mossy darkness memory
more real than anything
anything that ever was in all
the world and they shall
find at least these bodies broken against
no fact and no dream

b   a lamb in the distance

On the reality of loss and tense
and the participation of loss and tense
where loss is an imagined real
and tense may break in case
i. e.: as aorist breaks in instrumentals
dative garment and ablative
informant. Distinguish that the problem is not
of being and the dilemma is
not scalar and it is not differences
but distinctions that matter, for
there can be no avoirdupois
of location, nor metric of purpose except
as contingent to mensurand. As

death, an objective
and spasm.
Thus a present; the water-buckle and night
as a fist or from the local an express
        face pulls
away in the subway. There are
conversely, no rulers in instants,
for susceptibility to temporal position
is either habit or donation
and reveals primes,
gratuity and volition

c   *a time*

take one
from a pair a pair
from a quartet a quartet
from an
octet
the arrow through the octave
and the sun rising athwart
the ungloved thighs
the diamond refracted in honey
creep in thought
the minute spider creeps on the
eyeball the glass
rod swinging descends
ultimately to be
refracted in the pale
luminous solution
hair pulled by the wind
eyeballs flaked with light
the two princesses fall
from the ether of intensity
to the ether of irrevocables
and the yellow
animal climbs the cascade in the secret
interior of the highest
mountain

d

cause of a difficulty
trauma of the word
conflicts the eyes the clocks makes
morning pale makes artifacts
of cause so one a deep
so a single fact cool
one a person it was
then a time then and
a position not the same position
as formerly not the unknown
causes of slight cool being
not the cleave the borders
one pull the somatic anemone
or a person she interprets
this objectification as the interest
of a body being a place being
one a person a woman undertakes
this a thing an understood touched
artifact being more substantial
as having evolved out of
process and generality
not anticipated when
arrived not fully
understood

e

for an abrupt
conscious adjustment externalizes
shoulders instants and graces not
of a joy of being in one place and
then in another but of being
profoundly in one place thinking a
place internally
return to an irrevocable body
to the perpetuity of a death
to a gong in a dream

as there is a qualitative difference
between two stars, and a tightening
incline as result of thought
brilliant infinitesimals so now
undulant and cold this is displayed
as a field for a unique progress as a
quality of atmosphere measurable
and inescapable nothing can
forclose this crism nothing
can withstand for long memory
always awakens this usufruct
is held by a very old very endurable
meaning

THE THIN EDGE OF YOUR PRIDE

1922-1926

Poems for Leslie Smith

I

Later when the gloated water
Burst with red lotus; when perfect green
Enameled grass and tree, "I most solitary,
Boating," rested thoughtful on the moated water;
Where the low sun spread crimson
Interstices in the glowing lotus; aware
Of the coming, deep in the years, of a time
When these lagoons and darkening trees,
This twilight sliding mirror where we have floated,
Would surge hugely out of memory
Into some distant, ordinary evening—
Hugely, in vertigo and awe.

II

Six months as timeless as dream,
As impotent . . .
You pause on the subway stairs,
Wave and smile and descend.
Was it an instant between waking
And waking,
That you smile and wave again,
Two blocks away on a smoky
Chicago boulevard?
How many dynasties decayed
Meanwhile, how many
Times did the second hand
Circumvent its dial?

III

Indigenes of furnished rooms,
Our best hours have been passed
At the taxpayers' expense
In the public parks of four cities.
It could be worse, the level
Well-nurtured lawns, the uplifted
Rhythmic arms of children,
A bright red ball following
A graph of laughter,
The dresses of the little girls
Blossoming like hyacinths
In early August, the fountains,
The tame squirrels, pigeons
And sparrows, and other
Infinitely memorable things.

IV

Chill and abandoned, the pavilion
In Jackson Park stands like a sightless
Lighthouse beside the lake.
It is very dark, there would be no moon
Even if the night were not thickly overcast.
The wind moans in the rustic carpentry,
But the rain returns silently to the water,
Without even a hiss or a whisper.
We have the shadows to ourselves,
The lovers, the psychopathic, the lonely,
Have gone indoors for the winter.
We have been here in other autumns,
Nights when the wind stirred this inland water
Like the sea, piled the waves over the breakwater,
And onto the highway, tore apart tall clouds,
And revealed the moon, rushing dead white
Over the city.

V

The absorbent, glimmering night
Receives a solitary nighthawk cry;
Marshalls its naked housefronts;
And waits.
The lights of a passing yacht
Jewel for a moment your windblown hair.
The shadows of the lombardy poplars
Tilt like planks on water.
The sea breeze smells faintly of hospitals.
Far off,
On the desert coasts of the Antipodes,
Mountains slide silently into the sea.

VI

Paradise Pond

The minute fingers of the imperceptible air
Arrange a shadow tracery of leaf and hair
About your face.
Downstream a group of Hungarians from the mill,
Stiff with unaccustomed ease,
Catch insignificant fish.
A row of brown ducklings jerks itself across the water,
Moving like furry cartridges
Into some beneficent machine gun.
We shall arise presently, having said nothing,
And hand in vibrating hand walk back the way we came.

VII

I think these squalid houses are the ghosts
Of dinosaur and mammoth and all
The other giants now long rotted from the earth.
I think that on lonely nights when we,
Disparate, distraught, half a continent between us,
Walk the deserted streets,

They take their ancient forms again,
And shift and move ahead of us
For elbow room; and as we pass
They touch us here and there,
Softly, awestruck, curious;
And then with lurching step
Close in upon our heels.

VIII

"Whether or not, it is no question now,
Of time or place, or even how,
It is not time for questions now,
Nor yet the place."
The soft lights of your face
Arrange themselves in memories
Of smiles and frowns.
You are reading,
Propped up in the window seat;
And I stand hesitant at the rug's edge . . .
Whether or not . . . it is no question now.
I wonder what we have done
To merit such ironic lives.
Hesitant on the rug's edge,
I study the kaleidoscope
Before my toes, where some long
Dead Persian has woven
A cynical, Levantine prayer.

IX

After an hour the mild
Confusion of snow
Amongst the lamplights
Has softened and subdued
The nervous lines of bare
Branches etched against

The chill twilight.
Now behind me, upon the pallid
Expanse of empty boulevard,
The snow reclaims from the darkened
Staring shop windows,
One by one, a single
Line of footprints.

X

Out of the westborne snow shall come a memory
Floated upon it by my hands,
By my lips that remember your kisses.
It shall caress your hands, your lips,
Your breasts, your thighs, with kisses,
As real as flesh, as real as memory of flesh.
I shall come to you with the spring,
Spring's flesh in the world,
Translucent narcissus, dogwood like a vision,
And phallic crocus,
Spring's flesh in my hands.

XI

Someone has cast an unwary match
Into the litter of the tamarack woodlot.
A herd of silent swine watch the long flames
Blend into the sunset.
By midnight the fire is cold,
But long streamers of grey smoke
Still drift between the blackened trees,
And mingle with the mist and fireflies
Of the marsh.
I shall not sleep well tonight.
Tomorrow three days will have passed
Since I have heard your voice.

XII

After a hundred years have slept above us
Autumn will still be painting the Berkshires;
Gold and purple storms will still
Climb over the Catskills.
They will have to look a long time
For my name in the musty corners of libraries;
Utter forgetfulness will mock
Your uncertain ambitions.
But there will be other lovers,
Walking along the hill crests,
Climbing, to sit entranced
On pinnacles in the sunset,
In the moonrise.
The Catskills,
The Berkshires,
Have good memories.

XIII

This shall be sufficient,
A few black buildings against the dark dawn,
The bands of blue lightless streets,
The air splotched with the gold,
Electric, coming day.

XIV

You alone,
A white robe over your naked body,
Passing and repassing
Through the dreams of twenty years.

PHRONESIS

for Charles Henri Ford and Parker Tyler

I

And now old mammal, gall
He asked a question
He near and far asking
He said I must start at a place I remember and
    try and recall.
Fill that tube with blood and hold it to the light
    you will speedily see what was intended.
And what was discovered.
Of course certain rays won't penetrate.
Running a knife along the white edge of this cloister
    avoiding the crevices avoiding the results.
Void and void.
The proper and peculiar area begins here the defini-
    tions are a little frayed, it has been years but the
    partitions are capable of interlocking, the catharsis,
    narke, the flash on clash, narcosis, white white
    white the swift enveloping shutter. Pull everything
    to the retina wall. Follow the blue, it is very thin,
    speed, follow the blue, it is very thin, speed,
    follow the blue and the abrupt.
The motions are adjusted.
Retroactive and ambivalent.
After they had been fed and fattened they did with
    them as was the custom in that city. The blue
    and abrupt rocks. Sweet haltered lovely cast and
    quaver.
A plaster hand holding a speckled egg lay on a small
    sod overhead the four aluminum dirigibles and
    the sunlight the shadow about which there was
    no question.
A handful of battered vertebrae.
Chew, chew, broad flat dun squares.
It is a far away rattle and readjustment. The waves
    lap lap the shore stiffens on the hill the horses
    can be distinguished moving in the moonlight.

Bright exhalation in the evening.
If a man can.
Nobody can.
The shoulders shift, swift pain.
If you can tell where it leaves off. You can if you
    follow the chart closely. Cold water goes over
    granite. Snow falls. Pines revolve. And dull cuts
    the instep. The symbols are peculiar to this
    branch of the subject you will find them on the
    back. Now. See this is where the expiration oc-
    curred. This exhalation. Draying to be a light.
    You must be careful of what you eat.
Edges. Edges.
Lay it against your cheek and see how cool it is,
    how much returns.
Lorn dawn clear wrists of wind. Drawn over all that
    has intervened. Over the exploding lumber and
    the impenetrable spots. Think about sincerity.
    Do you suppose he was responsible for all that
    as they intimated.
Knowing much, dividing much from much.
Keep total arm and deep and ask.
They should look they haven't been exhausted by
    predecessors.
Muster. Drastic. The stars are easier. Lots of things
    are easier.
Watch for it as it comes round.
It just rattled through. It just hinged and clinked.
    Limped.
Slipped and tinkled.
It's over now and we didn't find it.
No we didn't find it.

                    II

Consular divides and the buttes glow.
The sagging noon.
We will color the pages grey olive beige and blue
    turning them slowly. We will break the backs of
    letters. There the snake whirrs.

The scoria omits nothing.
O fugitive ostrich-porcupine.
Peel tendon from tendon.
Are you intent, standing for everything. I am the
    only representative, the throb appeal, breaking.
Gasp and don't gasp, with your fists rub eyeballs
    and throat.
The mattresses lean against one another and the
    glass the doors are stacked.
It is very dusty up here the light comes in through
    the little holes, the slaughtered rectitudes lie
    around on the floor. The ink is brown.
A pool cue chalked makes a sound.
A discreet enervating squeak.
The old bones scale and chip.
A horse with one blue eye.
That is the color of the sky and the little lake.
    Black horse pursuing fracture. If you stop at
    the white hill top you will be among them. A
    chest and wedges war.
An olive tree grows there. Whenever they want to
    pick an olive they have to cut down the tree. It
    must be very inconvenient. So you would think
    but they don't seem to mind it.
Sometimes they go by awfully fast. You've got to
    jump in between.
I mean the aftermaths.
A white column and a white crescent. A lion gate,
    the shifting stone. The cabin smelled of iodo-
    form, the walls were covered with newspapers,
    rats ran behind them and made a terrific noise.
    The horses bumped against the porch all night.
    You used to sit in the purple shadow of a cluster
    of pines at the edge of the clearing, reading and
    sewing. They had orange trunks, forty feet to
    the first branches.
It is dawn in the markets, the polished fruits and
    vegetables, pink masts at the end of the streets.

III

Sometimes.

A sort of erasure.

That quality. That white. Mater Immaculata.

Lady. Stars.

Sometimes from behind glass that slips a little the
    face of a wax dummy cuts like a knife

Slicing a concentrated fecund curve

Think of Parmenides and a little glass box

A seamless glass box and a blue light

A silver plane a silver star the curve of an aluminum
    tube like a curve of fruit.

Intense pain makes mice sweat.

Occasionally when they operated on a man they left
    a snowball inside of him so now the snowballs
    have colored cords which hang down outside the
    incision. You can never use a snowball more
    than once so you might as well leave it in the
    patient but it is against the law.

For if the eye were an animal vision would be its
    soul, *i. e.* vision is the notional essence of the
    eye. The eye however is the matter of vision and
    if vision is wanting the eye is no longer an eye
    save in the meaning of a homonym, as a stone
    eye or a glass eye.

Soon the green will break into flame. Then it will be
    green no longer. It will be grey.

And the blue, will it always be blue.

Here one must apply a different standard. These forms
are not measured by time, for time is the clocking of
motion, the comparison of one motion with another, but
by the aeon, *aevum*, which is the form of their relation,
extraperipetal, to the celestial sphere. The internal relations
of the celestial sphere are, viewed as a whole, simultaneous.
From unique points within its manifold motion arises from
the reference of any one point or finite system of points to
the sum of their relations.

3 LOCAL MEN VANQUISH
MONSTER IN FIGHT

San Mateo, May 26. — A desperate but victorious 2-hour battle with a giant neurone in which knives flashed and boat gaffs and trout hooks were used as spears, was the thrilling experience today of Charles Small, Earl Ross, and Edward Holtz of this city.

The huge cephalopod, said to be the largest ever captured on the northern California coast is now on exhibition in a local sport shop. It was hooked by Small, manager of the Peninsular Parcel Delivery Co., while he and his two companions were fishing for rock cod 12 miles out at sea off Princeton.

It took the combined strength of the three men to bring the monster to the surface. Instantly, said Small, the air was filled with flying tentacles. They swished around like whips. One was cut off by Ross as it wrapped itself sinuously around Small's leg. Another tentacle was severed as it twined into the propeller. At one time the fishermen feared the fighting spider of the sea would capsize the boat.

The creature measured 12 feet in diameter. Deep sea experts say that 14 feet is the maximum size for Pacific coast neurones, altho few of this dimension have been found. The suckers on the tentacles close to the body measured one and one half inches in diameter.

It is uneven dust and dark.
Spit and dusty eye
At Mott Haven the subway has two levels. The
lower has a round roof and is very grey and full
of waste paper and the subway wind and the
subway smell. And a large black arrow. Negroes
get off and on there and go up and down.
A cold toe and a coffee steam.
A blurred window and a green lunch room.
A slopped marble counter and a slow sword.
Why is it like alkali water.
And an omen.

When the icicle breaks it will not be because I tried
     to look through it.
Second verse.
If you cry they will love you if you try they will be a
     little frightened.
If you sit too late by the cold water nobody will be a
     loser. If you *sculpe! limme! cisle!* the world will
     leap and bound about. They will love you. They
     will be tender and very neat.
When the cub reporter's buddy discovered atomic
     energy they left immediately for interstellar
     space. It was not until they landed on Mars that
     Dr. Fu Manchu emerged from the ice box.
Third verse. The hammer and sickle or Cut the
               Golden Bough.
Fourth verse. The assets deploy.
Consult the endeavor.
Prepare to.
Do not honor.
When the icicle breaks it will not be because I tried
     to look through it.
A darkness and no one to wonder.

Now drop like pencils the tubular bodies of the hosts
     of heaven.
Fra Angelico. Vacuum bottles of eternities these are
     the candles at your bier where you lie stiff and
     icy Sam Johnson there you lie thin and sunken
     all the idealists crying
Ineluctable modality!
Ineluctable modality!
The darkness behind the darkness.
We will introduce Mr. Longfellow to the coal pocket
     in the galaxy and the chamberlain of the court
     of the Duke of Brescia of 1349. Draw up a chair
     boys it's warmer over here. The neoplatonists
     like servants of the Fisher King bear past a
     flame enveloped object. Does anybody know
     what it is?

Nobody knows.
Here come the unreal children one by one children
   of the definite stars
So sweet their faces nonagonal paragonal and shin-
   ing. They stand in a row and sing.
Good morning dear teacher
Good morning to you
They join hands and dance and as they dance ring
   around the rosie the rosie appears, a monstrous
   pellucid pie. Slowly the lid lifts disclosing a
   moil of small animals live glass Christmas tree
   decorations, a few resemble Hawaiian fish. Some
   fly some hop some scamper some gasp for air.
   Then one by one they die and as they die they
   burst and as they burst it smells and when that
   happens all the children cry.
The hero enters. He is tall thin with platinum cheeks
   and muscles of steel. He inspects Sam Johnson,
   signs him with a rapid triple blessing. Johnson
   grows like a movie flower, in slight jerks, fat
   and rubicund. Just before he comes to life Long-
   fellow (smiling) the Chamberlain (asleep) the
   angels, archangels, principalities, powers, virtues,
   dominations, thrones, cherubim, seraphim,
   (looking chilled) the children (who have
   turned to plaster of paris, very white) all dis-
   appear in a noisy smoke. The neoplatonists rush
   through pursued by the Magna Mater.

IV

Rain falls on her glyptic eyelids
Beauty of vectors dies young and fair
A cleft altimeter hangs in the air
Caution. Between the smooth columns a drowse of
   colored paper falls.
A logarithmic spiral. I refer to the aforesaid aluminum.
A crimson ⊥ presses into the asphalt.

Intense pain makes mice sweat.

The mind, confined in this way to the definition,
     is seen to be epiphenomenal

Beneath the gold fillings of his teeth are secreted in-
     fernal machines but his voice is mild.

Mild hands the mild wash of mild seas on mild
     coasts mile on mile.

An orange **T** it is that emerges from the intersections
     and a blue **⊣** that creeps aimlessly about at the
     end of the streets.

And the neurones crawl over the paper. The paper
     crackles and it is wrinkled.

The young girls spin until they become invisible.

The subatomies of her despair cohere.

Day breaks, the breaking plates.

The three pale lights.

Smoke suspends in water.

The ostensive calm where the glaciers have always been.

It is dawn on the strained faces of the maidens who
     have been up all night

The sea is tendoned with electric herrings the prey
     of vast gulls.

The mountains are the color of the crows that flee
     from them screaming.

The flesh is thin on her cheeks like paper. Those
     who arrive will be confounded in her pale eyes.
     The grey swords will pass nothing will be
     asked of her they go to the unendurable torso
     and the gnawing mice.

The unbelievable cancer rises against the stars.

It is dawn in the valleys of the moon.

Your teeth. The breaking bones of your wrist and knee.

THE PLACE

for Yvor Winters

Unique planets break
the passing light
the serrate west the rose
graph oscillate and climbing
spark Antares needle and omen
germinate the apical blue
final crystal and absorbent
the thought
extends
secrets bloom
the bell wethers entangled in the waxen brush
the herd climbs out of dust
water speaks
cautious glockenspiel enshroud
nighthawk and bat
the grey herd bubbles
over the edge of the bench
meanders in the jackpine shadows
the Basquo's face spurts light
lambs stumble to calling ewes
the Basquo chews
speaks of Santander
of Yakima in winter
all night sheep speak intermittently
close at dawn
Utter bounty
after voluntary limit
cautiously anticipating
the single cosine
unambitious ballistics
minute focus
asymptotic object
before the fracture of the unsuspected calyx
or star
or haline signature

45

or the pinion that bloomed in the eclipse
unrequested
or crocus beneath oak leaf
Fabrics diadems spangles
the noetic flesh
the ivory minoan diver
this curve
this tensile promise
fusile apostle
lucent somatic crystal
beneath purple hemlock
the law of freedom
cloth of gold
lily and lotus
Hermetic invisible
eyes pause between invisible
pillars suspended above the white
table

> And as they went on their journey they
> came toward evening to the river Tigris,
> and they lodged there. And when the
> young man went down to wash himself, a
> fish leaped from the water and would have
> devoured him. Then the angel Raphael
> said unto him, Take the fish. And the
> young man laid hold of the fish and cast it
> upon the land.

the lamp
or eye
Even the trough
even the closing scissors
where the northern boar
bled in the broken wall
the helmets turned slowly green
amongst the flat stones
The further room
the root of light
the staff

given in the asian night
carried across Europe
planted in Glastonbury
the unguent
broken on the hair
Bread figs cheese olives grapes wine
the swords rest
mustered for war on the field of law
glories of kingdom
or lord of herds
and these
objects
the plume of mimosa
brushing the roof

CONFUSION

for Nancy Shores

I pass your home in a slow vermilion dawn,
The blinds are drawn, and the windows are open.
The soft breeze from the lake
Is like your breath upon my cheek.
All day long I walk in the intermittent rainfall.
I pick a vermilion tulip in the deserted park,
Bright raindrops cling to its petals.
At five o'clock it is a lonely color in the city.
I pass your home in a rainy evening,
I can see you faintly, moving between lighted walls.
Late at night I sit before a white sheet of paper,
Until a fallen vermilion petal quivers before me.

FUNDAMENTAL DISAGREEMENT
WITH TWO CONTEMPORARIES

for Tristan Tzara & André Breton

1

> "From any event intervals radiate in
> all directions to other events, and the
> real and imaginary intervals are sepa-
> rated by a cone which is called the
> null-cone."

gonaV

;
ing   evIT
  dras   pRoG
          2m3nL½
        pros
     *proS
instoting
tismaD
PROXY
gela
   domi
      immoderate
PROSPECT
savours curve doing instant conceptual bipartite
          engine
West inclination 32
PERSPECTIVE
engine
ENGINE
MACHINE
CONCEPTUAL PERSPECTIVE ENGINE
   x   y   z
motor-organ-organ-motor-......................ds!
number here
$\sqrt{2}$ to the left   to the right
distribute

origin of vector
description of vectors
the personal pronoun
vvvvvvvvvvvv
  vvvvvvvvvv
   vvvvvvvv
       v
i
modulatepersistendurereverserevolvereciprocate-
  oscillateperpetuate

ARRIVE

or pressure of significance
there exists an a
there exists an i
there exists at least one other entity b
valid
efficient
potent
which vests the prospect with originative continuity
the dominative pervasive accomodation of aspect
as the insertion localized as integer formaliter
thus acquiring trajectory
thus assimilating contingency
or the contingent as hiatus in the populous
meaning fused with recipient
amplitude coexists with discretion
importance endures with intervals
concentric and unique
not pendant
as an exterior
without contour
without projective meaning
shift digit
for this the fundamental number
of momentum
of retrograde traction
or of ingress
incarnate
tenuous

fluent
for this ophidian throat
twilight under the eucalyptus
stones sabers clouds kings nights leaves wishes
    arbors sparks shells wings mouths stars oranges
    fabrics ewes queens skins vehicles accents seeds
    cinders chutneys mixtures fevers apes eggs
    corpses mosses boxes shades irons glaciers
go up as if to be in or on
contemplate acumen distinguished as a formation
or the inane as mother of density
where the embassy of acquisition scrutinizes the
       monitor
or the spoon out of the sessile rainbow slides to the
      left of the mountains we are so prone to leave
      out of our calculations

    2

"The sea cucumber when in danger of being eaten, evis-
    cerates itself, shooting out its soft internal organs as a
    sop to the enemy while the body wall escapes and is
    able to regenerate a new set of viscera."

a

Profoundly and in state as casualty
the confusion lowered in
the reversible cross, the lowered
white cross thrust, glass baubled
integer in foam embroidery,
visual pollen seething between
the lashes, each focussed tendon
sown with eye bloom, each crowded
lily laminated with voracious
mouths. Ominous
the distinct difference. Lethal
the cleft intention. The flesh
motor in fog. The carnivorous
fungus of unpictured scene.

The gifts: a little cloud
a soiled handkerchief crumpled in a ball
the rose in alcohol
the brussels sprout in a sabot.
Electric and furry, that thing
hides in some worn
anonymous viscera, and now
summer being ended, the clocks
bulge, the liquescent
bulbs drop from the boughs, and splash
pale in the starlight on the stone.
That is your ambush, your gift, for your heels
will slide in the dark, your frosted onion
crash, its myriad capsules explode
ordure over the environs.

b

Now the hammock sword ensnares the febrile tree
palms ungloving haste across the sky
bloom veils off the wooly cormorant and race
of eye against returning
spears. So slice recurring
value, the spinner slicing
the red sphere concurs in taps
grounds soon and offers
which scattered crow or a blue sphere.
Revealing neither the arteries
of a fist nor peeling the iliac fascia.
A green bar
indifferent to imposition
reluctant as cruciform
cold as laminated, discovers
the horse wedge hammered
in crepuscular wind, or toss-pebbles
at night, late.
It was delivered in chunks and piled all over
at the end there was a termite left alone at the top
Should the honey comb

tossed from the rail of the liner
sink slowly
down
beyond the reach of the sun's rays
lower than life
which is impossible.

c

Glitter ghost
flame death as rose blossom
the poinsettia smashed in night.
Once late between the graves
the dogs sitting in a circle
waiting in the grey sand
o narthex, narthex
the crescents broken everywhere.
The chinaman in the dawn hurried
north between the mountains.
The second day, before light, the dome
flamed, the boy
spoke of the sea
and something ancient in a white casket.
Then appeared
like a seal through a paper hoop
the scarlet egg of the lunation
roaring through the sky
uprooting the brass trees
passing noiselessly
over the deserted cities
over the ghosts in nickel shrouds
over the moss green and purple headlands
over the grey sea.
The children approach the hyena diffidently
they approach the guardian of embers
the sky filled with red hands
the wind heavy with dry salt
o narthex
broken on the walls

d

As from the citron kelp untangling in the purple bay
only brain caryatids return
hands jewelled with seeds
only the red dog circles the rocks
so from the ivory cautiously the spatulate question
intrudes, mutters itself, branches in the room of souls.
So the oak leaves, whittled in copper
parade death and astonishment
so, carefully as an animal in a dream, blue
with an icy pelvis
unaware of secrets, the chronometer
bursts, first crimson, in the triangle
of Leo, then orange
in the belt of Orion.
The grey larvae of the oak leaves
spill voluminously out of the proscenium.
Mackerel hang in the waterspout.
And eyelids are shorn like foreskins
in this religion
and the wand is weighted with eyeballs
and the ice cream skull weeps
that never should have stayed
that will never leave.

e

How shall the stars on the cheeks
of this mandrill find a number.
They have seen stars as intervals.
They have broken the vermilion legs of the jungle.
They wait
the owl
the moth
the tower in flames
the ibis with multiple moist paps.
None other waits.
The cross gouged in the hummock

waits like a trap.
Over the white trees the stars
iris out in the sky
metallic breaths cross the air
and distinct against the dry grass
the black bears
the red baboons
wait, and the little girl
so pale, so fragile waited
naked, whispering to herself.
In the ravines the pilgrims foundered in the mire
their jaws were broken, they died
and lay unburied.

THE SUFFICIENT

for Louis Zukofsky

ancre ridgedge et poissoble gongpoint
(or) KAniv ubiskysplice ubi danAe ubi diamondane
thru oat quiv   at place
at daybreak   shellbreak
as an act so many nerves so many kilowatt hours
and this locus mallet
sempiternal bomb
history is not independence
after the dialectic
the international
concatenation is not immanence
unable to escape stung to somatic
death by the innumerable
hypodermics
: so death :
"the dog
swims close to earth"
and the yucca bloom from his shoulders
the perennial

aseity donated
each anniversary or immediate
transfinite the dark
nebula given
to the anvil improved
instrument not
doubt or the voracious
well where through a telescope
the soles of chinamen can dimly
be discerned
as
per se and paradigm
nor take place
but posit nor ask needles
of april for a stone this stone (those
calculi) or aurora this
web and thread or silver
crest million grunions
or vegetable strand governor
important not doubt
the cauliflower
doubts and grows
doubting
no firecracker
but insisting source and symbiosis
the myth that is true
a se
stoned in the synagogues
patronized by the occult
but the word
this and this as quality
fountain and fountchart
only its metric transcends
as value this gratuity
verb home
all verbs transitive
in the dative presence
and itself mirrored
invariant as grace, as the answer
plenum

INTO THE SHANDY WESTERNESS

for William Carlos Williams

Do you understand the managing.
Mornings like scissors
Leaves of dying.
Let event particle e. Point track m-n.
Cooling grey slender ascenders.
Congruence. Yes? that's what you thought it would be?
A flag waves, a kite climbs. Clouds climb, advancing
　　　impalpable edges.
The whole mottled sky turns slowly on its zenith,
　　　the same clouds go round and round the
　　　horizon.

As A is.
A triangular chessboard squared in two tones of grey,
　　　P to K3, KN x B.
It's very cold under the table. A cold window.
When he was little he used to go out to the barn
　　　and put his cheek against a cow and cry and
　　　cry. When he swam in the pasture creek the
　　　little fish tickled his legs.
Something is going to cut.
Something is going to break.
I don't see it I can't hear it but it's swinging.
One goes swiftly back. One goes forward. Two move
　　　to the left. A voice.
The steel column bores and bores into the ground.
　　　Presently the air is filled with ammonia fumes.
We will sing hymn number 366, "Art thou weary,
　　　art thou languid," 366
MY number, MY bleeding number. So I ups and
　　　tells em Why I was weary Why I was languid.

As B is.

Orange green yellow blue red violet.

Is there anybody there said the stranger. Is there
any reason why after all these difficulties we
should be subjected in this particular humili-
ating manner.

Orange. Row after row of shining minute faces.
Green. A slight lurch and then the floor begins
to climb smoothly steadily up up everything
clatters against the altar. The celebrant is em-
barrassed. White discs fly from the cylindrical
heads of the spectators and disappear out of the
windows. Presently only their palpitating necks
are left, hollow, dark purple inside.

It's pleasant to think of the cottages along the moun-
tainside. The alfalfa ripening in the afternoon.
The thin smoke of evening. The chill nights.

Assorted solutions, neat packages of peace were dis-
tributed by officious archangels. There was
much unemployment, long breadlines every-
where in the dusty cities, quiet, no traffic,
much patience. We came on, collecting visas,
wasting our substance in bribes, asking, Who
is king in this kingdom, who is your ruler,
by what do you measure?

Whenever I think of England I see Wyndham
Lewis standing in a high freezing wind on the
plain where Mordred and Arthur fought,
dressed only in his BVD's painfully extracting
thorns from his chapped buttocks. It grows
dark rapidly.

When I think of France I see Marcel Duchamp on
Michigan Boulevard in a raccoon coat and a
number of young americans praying before a
roller-coaster from which middle-aged french-
men strapped to bicycles leap into tubs of cocacola.

Now the blue flowers return the gravel mornings.
Now the immaculate mistresses
And those we loved from afar.
It's yellow in the sunlight and blue around the
      corner and it's all been so simple. The grey
      furry plants and the white hands. The consid-
      erations, the ablatives. The conversation about
      death. The lace parasol.
He was naturally very neat.
He was particular about neckties and very proud of
      his razors. They gleamed on maroon plush.
      His watch lost sixty seconds every four weeks
      neither more nor less. He sat on the screen
      porch smelling faintly of citronella and spoke
      slowly and distinctly of love. Then he died.
      And she hadn't made up her mind. So she
      walked under the lace parasol avoiding the de-
      cayed catalpa blossoms that littered the sidewalk.

It grows dark. A shitepoke flies up from the canal.
      That's a shitepoke he says to the boy. For
      supper hassenpfeffer. The rabbits are getting
      at the tomato sets, bad. Tourists are camping
      down at the woodlot at the corner. You can see
      their fire from the back door. When they came
      for water Nero snapped at the man. Now he
      looks over at their fire and barks every few min-
      utes. On both sides of the walk about every ten
      feet all the way to the gate bushel baskets are
      turned upside down over the peonies. As it
      gets darker they disappear.

MEMORANDUM

for Horace Gregory

If distraught shall be the word or not,
Or understanding, or misunderstanding,
Terror, no not, or any glazed thing,
Impervious or treacherous, as final
And distraught before the last, the bright
Consumate flower. And he the sensual
And the dark rebel, bound now outward,
Gone out haunted by the quincunx of heaven,
By Fomalhaut and pulsing Algol,
By Orion and the dim thick nebula,
Observed by the indifferent eye
Of the cassowary, the understanding
Crimson nostrils of sharks in tepid
Bright oceans, and distraught, stoned by fetishes,
Or dead, and the grave marked with an oar,
Vibrating in the wind till the next spring tide,
The pale sea collapsing sleepily,
Booming on the shingle in the sun filled fog
Distraught by the inorganic eye
Of the jerking squid, the irrefutable stare.
Or restless nights unwashed and thirsty,
Sleeping among the stones and alkali dust,
The dwarf owls barking from their burrows.
Or distraught, terror within and the sword without,
A hundred miles of wind driven sand,
The fuel exhausted, the cold freezing the eyes.
Statistics. Kisses. Assassins. Bombs.
Pricing and weighing. Parting and being born.
Distraught or not, the iron at the throat.

DEATH, JUDGMENT, HEAVEN, HELL

The functioning total then,
Metabolic or catabolic,
Posits the geminal unit —
Position, created encapsulate —
The marvelous onion exploding
In successive exfoliations
Of purpose, falling away
In the primary discourse,
The resolution of vector tension —
He loves me, he loves me not.
　　Where the Bighorn scrambles over the snow
And disappears and the glaciers
Are a little smaller each year,
Where during an eclipse of the moon
A great white owl flew over the icefields
Calling like a bell.
　　　　　　　　　　Transparent granules
Radiate over the brain, leaving a path
Of glimmer behind like slugs in the evening.
The evening disappears in the sky
Over the basalt beach. They have lost something
Amongst the ferns and she stands
Holding a lantern while he searches
On hands and knees.
　　　　　　　　There is a slight wind
Which always arises from the opposite
Shore when the water has become white
In the evening.

　　　　The geminal unit —
If you can find the street you will find
No difficulty in finding the shop
Where they sell little boxes of ashes.

Each leaf is an encyclopedia
Slowly reading itself, keeping
Inviolate the secret of its
Discrimination, falling slowly
Through the counter-glow of which it is a part.

Beyond Neptune the beckoner
Is known to pass, as birds seen falling
Skyward in the water's mirror
Transmute that curved opening in space
To song. Weighted, neural transversals
Gather against the bone, thus, explode and fuse
Thus, and leave their spoor like dinosaurs
In that quick lime.

So rises in the
Responsibility of achievement
The idea of birds, the theorem
Of the wing, the transit of the sphere—
Rising against the net of dark the bright
Planes, the shadows jangling in a crackle of light.
On the last ellipse the loadstone passes;
The iron falls in the night; the cloven
Merges; the focus whirls in the gulf;
The curve of grace spreads, remembering
Over the contour of the vase
The tangent creeping *ultra Herculis Columnas.*

THE CRISIS

for Dorothy Van Ghent

I

earth upon earth
between the confines of the day
and night earth took
of earth the careful clay of earth
compound with wrong and all woe
saying war
death destruction in these hands I bear
and form from the war
of earth and earth fear
on the irremediable ways
earth hypocrite to trusted earth
the faithless sky
the sly sea offer only
the old lie
a naked corpse tossed by nameless waves
earth in the earthen urn thrown
now the howling dogs advance in glimm'ring
light now earth in fogs falls stumbling
at last to earth and we falling
in dazed sleep drunken
surfeited with earth
wandering in the waste
dominion of birth
know of earth
little nor how nor why

II

What the Stars Say and A Prayer to the Stars

They wish, that they may also perceive things. Therefore,
they say that the star shall take their heart, with which they
do not a little hunger, the star shall give them the star's heart,
the star's heart, with which the star sits in plenty. For the

star is not small, the star seems as if it had food. Therefore, they say, that the star shall give them of the star's heart, that they may not hunger.

The stars are wont to call, "Tsau, Tsau." Therefore, the Bushmen are wont to say that the stars curse them the springbok's eyes, the stars say "Tsau, Tsau." I am one who was listening to them. I questioned my grandfather, what things it could be who spoke thus. My grandfather said to me that the stars were the ones who spoke thus. The stars were the ones who said, "Tsau" while they cursed the people the springbok's eyes. Therefore, when I grew up, I was listening to them. The stars said, "Tsau, Tsau." Summer is the time when they sound. Because I used to sleep with my grandfather, I was the one who sat with my grandfather, when he sat in the coolness outside. Therefore, I questioned him about the things which spoke thus. He said the stars were the ones who spoke thus, they cursed the people the springbok's eyes. My grandfather used to speak to Canopus, when Canopus had newly come out he said, "You shall give me your heart, with which you sit in plenty, you shall take my heart, with which I am desperately hungry. That I might also be full like you. For, I hunger. For, you seemed to be satisfied, hence you are not small. For, I am hungry. You shall give me your stomach, with which you are satisfied. You shall take my stomach, that you may also hunger. Give me also your arm, you shall take my arm, with which I do not kill. For, I miss my aim. You shall give me your arm. For, my arm, which is here, I miss my aim with it." He desired that the arrow might hit the springbok for him, hence he wished the star to give him the star's arm, while the star took his arm, with which he missed his aim. He shut his mouth, he moved away, he sat down, while he felt that he wished to sit and sharpen an arrow.

from Bleek—Bushman Texts

III

the sky turns violet
o you friend
the earth turns violet
o you friend
only the wind blows
o you friend
only the small birds flown
o you friend
from behind the disc of the sun
the rays of the sun pull groaning
pull groaning why o why
delay so long o lord of lords
for the lamb fallen in the herd shall I look
shall I look for the small lamb lost from the herd
shall I look o you friend
for the young ram stumbled in the herd
o you friend
for the ewe lost from the herd
o you friend
shall he take the bow
he of the sure eye the strong one
shall he take the axe
he of the sure arm the strong one
o you friend
shall he take the noose
he of the sure wrist the strong one
o you friend
this is the shining day of his advent
the clear-eyed the bright haired one
o you friend.

from Seligman—The Veddah

64

IV

Constable of the singular hearts that appear
Beaded with smoke on the confines, the meanders
Of a night of small discreet flares
And dragonish twilight, she met you carrying
The pastries of inferno heaped in a tray
Upon your head. "Be seated in a wilderness"
She said, "and tell me your story."
You smiled, produced the covert omen,
The mangled segilla she had feared.
Her fingers splayed in the moss and through the trees
Behind her filed the white lewd hypocrites
One by one, emaciate and nude.
A freight train growled on a far
Edge, moaned at a crossing where fireflies
And cat tails were. She advanced a silken leg,
A hand beringed and aqueous, against
Your thigh. She said, "Your cheeks are polished tin
Your eyes, the restless larvae of your brain
Feed in my bones. See how the meteors, falling
Are reflected in your forehead, stream
In the sky and course above your eyebrows.
That force is yours to use, compulsion
Is your inheritance." She leaned near,
Breathed in your nostrils. We saw you then
Press a stiff hand to your rigid eyes, open
Your lips and close them silently again,
Arise, pulse like a spring against a weight
And go to where the chalk-eyed man of small
Machines waited your bargaining.
She followed, caressing your hands, weeping
A little, begged you wait, saying
"Beware the forest horror stops
You where the paths cross. The guillotine
Animal crouches on the low branches,
Clockwork terrors tick in the bushes, and the moon's
Light falls slice by slice without pause
Without mercy. Dare you go there
Alone?" We heard your answer "I have gone

Where only the sea moved. I have moved
Painfully over the ancient mud.
Where the silent kingdoms
Of the luminous fishes swept like swift
Constellations a mile above. Only the sea
In large blocks moving in the years,
And the bones of drowned men
Picked clean in passage circling down."
She said, "I know and I am satisfied
We trust each other. Let us go."
The chalk-eyed pedlar rose as you approached
Hunched his back and wet his lips. You showed
Your little silver. He nodded
Sympathized and looked askance, at last
Sighed and fished in his pack, produced
A gyroscope, a coffee grinder, a saw,
A carburetor, an easy death, a patent trap,
Six obvious absolutes. Six candidates
Storming your Pantheon in a little row.
You watched him wrap them in an old newspaper
Counted your change, returned his bow,
And paced the wind along the forest aisles,
She gliding lambent by your side.
Presently the blind persistent moles
Crept sleek from the earth, black
In the moonlight, and devoured
The pastries lying on the ground.

V

The great year climbs the blackened sky,
The whirling equinoxes close their term,
The moon turns to the earth her unknown face.
Loneliness—
The flesh and the bones ragged with wounds.
Where have the chanting litanies wound away?
What flaring visions burn out day?
Let the luminous vaults of the sequoia
Resound with song of this last splendid bird.
Announce the climacteric convocation,

The passages and the conflagrations
And here mark out in air a sphere for wings
And drive away tamed spayed fates and furies.
Prohibit the ritual meek physician
Thumb shuttering eyelid forefinger to lip
And every overstuffed iota, every
Amoebic despot deprive of passport.
Let only the regal dream, the magniloquent
Geometric abstract emperor come near,
Let the ending only song fracture the long
Throat made supple with a lifetime's silence.
Let the maimed with age the clay eyed mourner
Go away weeping each in his own midnight,
For now the conjunct dual flame speeds toward
The whirling corolla of the eclipse.
Giver and receiver at last are one.
Vision roars in the loud forge of dream
And over the translucent surface
Of the molecule sweep the glimmering
Shadows of planets moving
Within its hot entrails.
Enumeration decayed in that benignity,
No integer between Polaris and the Southern Cross,
All victory placeless in that ubiquity,
Sown with mirrors fire drenched
Beyond possession beyond meaning,
This duality had devoured
The bowels of a promethean logic
And now at the end after the many
Failures and catastrophes, from the rock
Rang out the shuddering voice of the victim,
Wrung from the glutted trunk, ripping the air.
Finally monad and triad,
All your secret tireless principles,
Shrink to a last ember, and the jawbone
Pulverizes, the teeth seed furrowed soil.
Seventy years thought froze the fontanelles,
Sancta Sophia has crashed at last
Only a few gold wires thread the dust
Of all those singular embroideries,

The wheel swings on itself and wavers to a stop.
Neither history nor genesis forever now,
Though such a truth as may
Shall spread its words on walls
And such a beauty may coquette
From gauze thigh and red lip,
From now henceforward
All midnights wait,
The head in the hands,
The urn upon the knee.

OKEANOS AND THE GOLDEN SICKLE

for R. E. F. Larsson

Where is the toothed estuary the toothed
Wave, the ancient expense of fog-pale
Green water, that she should move
So sure in brittle languor
Over serrate sand? That she
Should never sing? Let us forget
The white drawn lips, the watery
Weak flesh. Ah lady, draw the long
Throated violins, the occult single bell
Nearer that we may pluck
Old music in an unknown wind.
Why should she tread the opulent
Promenade, the long avenue
Of narrow trees with so tired
Grace, with such immorally
Instinctive ease?
Give over ivory keys
And ominous untroubled
Drums and let the music be
Sharp, and friable, and somehow
Softer than the old elementalisms.

WHEN YOU ASKED FOR IT

for Frances Prudhomme

Dear Friend,

.....the day the seal came up the beach and
mother fed him fish from the porch of the cottage all the
children were away on a hike. However, when we went to the
mountains the snow was just melting off the highest valleys
and when it left it left carpets of yellow snow lilies with fragile
watery stems. They say the deer eat them but we didn't see
any, only tracks. They were timid for the trappers had just left
the month before and in this locality these gentlemen are not
adverse to killing a deer now and then for meat in the long
winter. And there were whistling coneys that whistled almost
a tune, we saw lots of them, and porcupines, and once an old
bear sat up across the canyon and looked at us for quite a
time, he sat so still nobody saw him until John whispered,
"Theres a bear across the canyon looking at us, sh-h." The
girls had to scream but that didnt faze him, he kept right on
looking, and after a while he got tired and went away. We
used to bathe in the creeks which flowed right off the snow,
and was it cold. The fishing was poor and we didnt see many
birds but the fir trees stood up all around with a beautiful
taper and ever so slightly purplish . . . .

In the evening by the flowers
In the evening by the green bronze
Trickle of watered wines the blossoms purple lips
And the wind and the wool of the surf blown
    diminishing in over grey sand
Star in the east
Star in the west
Wish that star was in my breast
Entomological emperor
Master of the insect catalog
The long narrow white pages and the legs many
    jointed pasted down with little bands of trans-
    parent paper

Gone
Some of these days
Gone
Some of these days
Gone
Some of these days
Gone
Some of these days
Gone
Gone
Knowing
That is knowledge
That is hard a hard mystery
Even Father Orkings doesnt know
Beyond the windward horizon lie beds of weak flowers
They are crushed in places and in places the rain
   has beaten them into the sand
They are white and it is evening
We have instant death
Some of these days I am going to throw myself
     up for grabs
Alum
Alum pencilled on the cheeks
And the right angles that go in opposite directions
   the grey light the yellow barred windows
(wanted and wanted)
The air filled with flying hands
A stack of china about to fall
Eyes in the ice
Teeth
And the lines recede
There is nothing but receding lines and a cross
   in electric lights
There is a flayed airplane

The axe was deeply imbedded when I tried to lift
        it out of the encyclopedia a shudder of pain crept
        out on my diaphragm and then then they
        crawled out of its white flaky flesh hundreds of
        them and then I wanted to pull wool I wanted
        to pull wool along spines
I know quiet
Weir
I know old fences
Some of these days
Gone eyes
Air
When you asked for it did you get it
Were they many
Were they hard
Put the T square there
The triangle there and the compass
Sift the evening
And the filmy filmy smoke
Pink and grey
Question the subaltern
Question the beautiful delicate lady
You know what she means to you
Silver and saffron all slick and tinkle
She leans on the arm of the master physicist
He wears a leather jacket and his face is silver
He draws question marks rapidly on the backs of
        envelopes

                        (are you there)
Are you waiting for us patiently as you said you would
And did you get it
Do you know do you believe do you transpire do you
Come to color
Relieving capture and devolving arc
Intransitive

This is not for us this is for the people down the
    street with the same name they have a little
    boy they dress him in very clean wash suits
    and he sings all day
Intransitive
Come to color
Between the edge of cube and cube the twilight
    thickens day deserts the eastward windows the
    cypress groves along the westward sea
Come to color and devolving arc
Claws are rapid clutch is rapid big figures
    walk past

                (the T square)
How white it is and how beautiful the lines look
On every roof is a flagpole thin tapering tipped
    with a black ball the fire escapes go swiftly up
    and down and the escaping firemen go
    swiftly up and down them
When you asked
They were many
There were a lot of bronze horses and marble
    goddesses and we saw we must walk very
    swiftly across this square and turn up the alley
    to the light in the doorway
Inside each shop a light burns above a cheap iron safe

                (are you there)
Hold my hand and keep out of the rushes
Nothing will hurt you everybody loves you and I
    want you to be very happy
She cried and said I've got to go I really ought
    to go
The master physicist
You mustnt do that he said we dont advise it it
    interferes with the work of the committees and
    interrupts the sessions of the congress
Goodbye o lady goodbye
When you asked for it

It is a little novel
We arranged a collusion
We arranged a beatified nisus
Leaping and washing the very dark place
O the lithe wavering wisp
Leaping and washing
There is always a procession of strange geezers
    just a little to the left and to the rear solemnly
    and very slowly going down many steps some-
    times they are around a corner or obscured by
    the thick trees
Where ever you go
Have you stayed so long by the sea watching the
    sun and the sand-pipers running along the edge
    of the water the sea weed rolling under the surface
Because he was an odd child
Try not to caper and call when the institutions
    are busy because nothing is more disagreeable
    than that half questionable activity in times
    of great strenuous searchings

Mary was her name
She was very neat very studious and inclined to
    affect chastisements
Question this endeavor
Mary are you enquiring
Herbert are you piercing the planks the cords the
    cubicles one after another
Name the series you have uncovered
The river was beautiful there at the sea mouth
    full of colorless intense light in the twilight the
    fog poured in from the sea between two of the
    lower hills small rodents appeared and disap-
    peared abruptly
Give me your hand
Herbert
Mary
Slowly obstructing the narrow valley the rectilinear
    ogre slowly

Devouring
She had not tried to make this an edge of the
    type demanded but she had hoped a lot of you
Clarion and clarion o so
Mary you know what it has been like
I do Herbert
Its a long evening the light lasts a long time
Everything is so quiet
I want you to uphold it though
True and the balances swinging
Do you know me at all
Close
There is too big a jump and too sure a requisition
Do long a sound bowling
Hands smoothing and smoothing
Right and right
Do

Am I a good woman
Who are you that you should wonder all the
    grass a wave it
The wire curls and curls slow
Greased green the thin kind line
Right cause to make much
I dont like the woods there are things under the roots
I tried and tried
Make fast there make fast
Mary we know what comes in at the deposition we really
    sympathize with you a lot
12345678
Nobody will help enough though the pressure is too great
I know I know

Doing this for us you blossom
Deter deter granting deter
Deter granting
Here I am
I have waited and wondered and thats all you have to say to me

Glass put the hand back
A long black middle creak
Dont gape
Hope and knowledge
Its your own fault though youre a fool and you know it
I certainly was
Take
Now there is one here see it off to the left and
    then you go that way along and cold cotton bale
    wet wood hope and hope hope and knowledge
Breathing little books and your gloves and your hands
But I dont wear gloves
Not even in winter
Not even in winter
Sometimes little vertigo sometimes little knowledge
Come near

Noise and night
I saw my sister in a white nightgown walking
    among purple tree trunks in a heavy fog very
    slow and with a gentle smile just like she was
    laid away
My brother died when he was ten years old he had
    dark red hair he died from a fall
Thats a big stone
Yes thats a big stone we are going to build a fire
    over it and then throw water on it sometimes the
    pieces fly a long way one killed a cow last
    spring a long sliver of granite
Right between the eyes

Deep moist walk
Tamaracks crack in the wind but not here it is
    quiet here with noises like night in the city
The hill slip
It wont do a bit of good it wont help
Hope and knowledge

Its been so difficult you cant possibly imagine how
    terrible it has been trying and trying and never
    getting anywhere and never knowing never
    being able to see it
Ive lacked attention for long construction
Its lonely and constant
Its dark now the trees look like teepees
Grey
Right between the eyes
Deep moist walk
O hold fast to me hold fast to me

We tried very hard to make it what we thought
    it had ought to be
Resilient sympathy and the hands
Walking together reading aloud in the evening
The green utterly beautiful twilight
The pistons rock and plunge it is very white there
    is an unshaded electric globe and one man in
    grey striped overalls far down on a gallery
    watches the slow movement of red and green
    lights across a board once in a great while he
    throws a switch and the fresh copper bars gleam
    for an instant
The heart beating and beating one feels it now the
    diaphragm slipping over undulant waves as
    one walks the abrupt shudder of peristalsis
He knows her lips all her little nerves her web
    of capillaries her capsules of mysterious fluids

Twilight
A number of people on a wide street
A palm turned upward at a table the marble cold
    against the back of the hand
Trout swimming in a window
The gold fillings in teeth
I get to thinking of him
When I see him I notice his socks need mending

My eyes ache and I have a confused headache

See them coming inexorably the narrow hooves of
their horses their voices hoarse with dust their
robes spectacular in the sunlight their swords
whirling above their heads

When a man has grown close to a woman and we
were so close

You had better ask the captain

But his splendor terrifies me he is all alone on the
bridge and the wind presses against him

Perhaps Ive hurt him terribly if I could only go
away I could forget about it but I see him all
the time and when I dont see him I worry
about him

I feel as though something were striking my face
with the edge of a hand vertically down the
center of my face and across my eyes

A door was opened in the ceiling and something
was poured into this room

Where is the cat

In the corner

There is an arrow here pointing up those long
stairs there is sweat on the walls

The old woman is a long way down the tunnel it
is difficult to see her because of the dust and
the imperfect illumination but she seems to be
picking up things and she is in a great hurry

I believe you can get out to the end of it if you
try of course its very frail

If I only had a little money

His pride

He is working across the river I know he doesnt
like his job there was so much he wanted to do
perhaps he can never recover a lot of the
things I am taking with me there is a lot I can
never recover

Blue veins beneath the chalky skin the bones
    showing through yellow the hair on the hands
    frizzled as though it had been singed
The leaves of the eucalyptus the leaves of the
    madroñe spin in the wind ferry boats crawl
    over the water and disappear behind the islands
    as the fog comes in a siren moans then another
Why dont you try a little harder why do you
    forget the things that were so important you
    used to be so careful

I need money so badly I could go away as it is Im
    caught out here it costs so much to live in New
    York when I dont see him I wonder how he
    is getting along what he is doing now
Maybe he is in his room reading maybe he is
    walking along one of those empty streets where
    the railroads cross one another walking and
    thinking
He needs me so much

There is a faint odor of burning oil the hissing
    and crackling of a long spark several lids slap shut
Stretch out your arm and strain your fingers wide apart
The graph looks like a row of canine teeth the
    gold leaf rises and falls charging and discharging
Dont worry about it dont think I mean everything
    I say it will be all right

IN WHAT HOUR

(1940)

"The next chapter is concerned with the puzzling fact that there is an actual course of events which is in itself a limited fact, in that metaphysically speaking, it might have been otherwise."

A. N. WHITEHEAD

FROM THE PARIS COMMUNE
TO THE KRONSTADT REBELLION

Remember now there were others before this;
Now when the unwanted hours rise up,
And the sun rises red in unknown quarters,
And the constellations change places,
And cloudless thunder erases the furrows,
And moonlight stains and the stars grow hot.
Though the air is foetid, conscripted fathers,
With the black bloat of your dead faces;
Though men wander idling out of factories
Where turbine and hand are both freezing;
And the air clears at last above the chimneys;
Though mattresses curtain the windows;
And every hour hears the snarl of explosion;
Yet one shall rise up alone saying:
"I am one out of many, I have heard
Voices high in the air crying out commands;
Seen men's bodies burst into torches;
Seen faun and maiden die in the night air raids;
Heard the watchwords exchanged in the alleys;
Felt hate speed the blood stream and fear curl the nerves.
I know too the last heavy maggot;
And know the trapped vertigo of impotence.
I have traveled prone and unwilling
In the dense processions through the shaken streets.
Shall we hang thus by taut navel strings
To this corrupt placenta till we're flyblown;
Till our skulls are cracked by crow and kite
And our members become the business of ants,
Our teeth the collection of magpies?"
They shall rise up heroes, there will be many,
None will prevail against them at last.
They go saying each: "I am one of many";
Their hands empty save for history.
They die at bridges, bridge gates, and drawbridges.

Remember now there were others before;
The sepulchres are full at ford and bridgehead.
There will be children with flowers there,
And lambs and golden-eyed lions there,
And people remembering in the future.

AT LAKE DESOLATION

The sun is about to come up and the regiments lie
Scattered in the furrows, their large eyes
Wet in the pale light and their throats cut.
At noon the plow shearing the purple loam,
And the hands of the plowmen, the blood
Black on the knuckles. He has asked.
He has seen the naked virgins and matrons
Impaled and disemboweled. He has asked.
He has seen water wafering
Over stones. He has asked. He has seen
The roan gelding break through the alkali crust,
Sink rampant in the fetid mud. He has asked.
Moving towards hot crepuscular horizons,
He has asked. He has seen the nude children
Run screaming. He has asked. Their eyes
Festering their nostrils scalded. He has asked.
The fermented pulp oozes through the rotting fruit skin,
The unborn phoenix screams within the breakfast eggs.
The horrible abundances, the little blind answers
Like maggots, the dukes on the towering moor
Benighted in their cardboard armor; and he,
Locked in the vertebrae of the Sierra, saw
The sharp alley of night, the trail
Glimmering and feet pausing and going
On beside him; and beyond the tangled
Thicket and the thorns saw
Hakeldama, the potter's field,
                    Full of dead strangers.

GENTLEMEN, I ADDRESS YOU PUBLICLY

*"No marvel though the leprous infant dye
When the sterne dam envenometh the dug"*
Edward III

They said no one would ever care
They said it would never make any difference
And after the years of waiting
I didn't it hadn't mattered originally
It didn't matter then
But why do they stand so
Why do they never go
What are they waiting for
What monstrous new planet
Glowing in a cloud of omen
Must appear poised on their red-hot alps
And now bolting from sleep
And unbelieving hearing
In the night echoing and reechoing
The glaciers walking or the midnight
Recurrent smashing of a train wreck
But nobody knows now
They said there were many
Before the wars
Now nobody cares
This knife is guaranteed to float on water
It's made for you take it it's yours
As you lie under the rocking stars on the organic
Vertiginous lift of the ocean
It will float out chill and sly
Creeping under the sternum in an inexplicable
Shiver nothing much will happen
The eyes half-open the hair floating
The starlight glittering on the moist teeth
They will remain the same
Only the heart and lungs will stop
But the breast will go on rising
Falling with the undulant ocean

Each night thereafter the corpuscular
Animation of the sea will shine more thickly
Until at last
Aureate and upright
Walking waist deep on the breaking combers
Some one screaming sees it from a boat

HIKING ON THE COAST RANGE

On the Anniversary of the Killing of
Sperry and Conderakias in the
San Francisco General Strike
Their Blood Spilled on the Pavement
Of the Embarcadero

The skirl of the kingfisher was never
More clear than now, nor the scream of the jay,
As the deer shifts her covert at a footfall;
Nor the butterfly tulip ever brighter
In the white spent wheat; nor the pain
Of a wasp stab ever an omen more sure;
The blood alternately dark and brilliant
On the blue and white bandana pattern.
This is the source of evaluation,
This minimal prince rupert's drop of blood;
The patellae suspended within it,
Leucocytes swimming freely between them,
The strands of fibrin, the mysterious
Chemistry of the serum; is alone
The measure of time, the measure of space,
The measure of achievement.
                      There is no
Other source than this.

A LETTER TO WYSTAN HUGH AUDEN

Frightening a Child

It's not wise to go walking in the ruin.
Lest they should fall the cracked walls are held with chain,
All the lintels are covered with willow shoots
And the stones have shifted in the winter rain.
Leave the gate unclimbed and with untampered seal,
There are much better places to take the air.
The broken mosaics are best left unseen,
The robin's eggs in the shattered clock unclaimed.

Others have climbed to the tower's top to wish,
And kiss the face carved there unobliterate,
And fallen or been robbed or drowned the same day.
The rocks that line the moat are sharper than steel
And keep the bones that plunged to calling voices.
Men have died there helpless in the gathering ice.
The arches are all awry that once held taut.

You've a future before you that's still unseen,
Let glories of exploration go unclaimed.
You can break some far more profitable seal
Than keeps out vagrants and keeps in wind and rain.
There's only trouble waiting in the ruin,
You're better off playing in the sun and air,
Or making wild salads out of bracken shoots,
Or weaving violets in an endless chain.

Advising an Adult

No wish to leave unseen
No day to pass unclaimed
The unobliterate seal
The steel rain

Voices in the old ruin
Flayed hands seen in the air
Ice black on the green shoots
The taut chain

85

REQUIEM FOR THE SPANISH DEAD

The great geometrical winter constellations
Lift up over the Sierra Nevada,
I walk under the stars, my feet on the known round earth.
My eyes following the lights of an airplane,
Red and green, growling deep into the Hyades.
The note of the engine rises, shrill, faint,
Finally inaudible, and the lights go out
In the southeast haze beneath the feet of Orion.

As the sound departs I am chilled and grow sick
With the thought that has come over me. I see Spain
Under the black windy sky, the snow stirring faintly,
Glittering and moving over the pallid upland,
And men waiting, clutched with cold and huddled together,
As an unknown plane goes over them. It flies southeast
Into the haze above the lines of the enemy,
Sparks appear near the horizon under it.
After they have gone out the earth quivers
And the sound comes faintly. The men relax for a moment
And grow tense again as their own thoughts return to them.

I see the unwritten books, the unrecorded experiments,
The unpainted pictures, the interrupted lives,
Lowered into the graves with the red flags over them.
I see the quick gray brains broken and clotted with blood,
Lowered each in its own darkness, useless in the earth.
Alone on a hilltop in San Francisco suddenly
I am caught in a nightmare, the dead flesh
Mounting over half the world presses against me.

Then quietly at first and then rich and full-bodied,
I hear the voice of a young woman singing.
The emigrants on the corner are holding
A wake for their oldest child, a driverless truck
Broke away on the steep hill and killed him,

Voice after voice adds itself to the singing.
Orion moves westward across the meridian,
Rigel, Bellatrix, Betelgeuse, marching in order,
The great nebula glimmering in his loins.

ON WHAT PLANET

Uniformly over the whole countryside
The warm air flows imperceptibly seaward;
The autumn haze drifts in deep bands
Over the pale water;
White egrets stand in the blue marshes;
Tamalpais, Diablo, St. Helena
Float in the air.
Climbing on the cliffs of Hunter's Hill
We look out over fifty miles of sinuous
Interpenetration of mountains and sea.

Leading up a twisted chimney,
Just as my eyes rise to the level
Of a small cave, two white owls
Fly out, silent, close to my face.
They hover, confused in the sunlight,
And disappear into the recesses of the cliff.

All day I have been watching a new climber,
A young girl with ash blond hair
And gentle confident eyes.
She climbs slowly, precisely,
With unwasted grace.
While I am coiling the ropes,
Watching the spectacular sunset,
She turns to me and says, quietly,
"It must be very beautiful, the sunset,
On Saturn, with the rings and all the moons."

THE MOTTO ON THE SUNDIAL

It is September and the wry corn rattles
Dry in the fields. It is dawn, the spider webs
Are white in the tracks of the cattle, the holes
Where they have torn up the grassroots, they are
Dry, sticky, no dew is on them. The morning
Comes, it is hot with the first dawn and windless.
The floury dust in the cowpath curls over no
Higher than my boot top and then settles
Into my crumbling footprints. The torn crows settle
Again into the dead elm, saying little.
MacGregor, Iowa. I stand on the bluff
Looking out over the river, the water
Oozing past and the smell coming up from it,
Up from the scabby flat where the pigs stumble.
In Wisconsin smoke blooms over the forest,
Plumed at first and then flattening slowly.
I have seen the fog over the lotus beds,
White, curded and thick to the bluff's edge, the sun
Yellow over Wisconsin and the sky blue,
The air wet and jewelweed in the ravine,
Wet, and the colored sandstone like wet sugar.
It is later than you think, fires have gone over
Our forests, the grasshopper screamed in our corn,
Fires have gone over the brains of our young girls,
Hunger over young men and fear everywhere.
The smell of gas has ascended from the streets,
Bloomed from the cartridges, spread from wall to wall,
Bloomed on the highways and seeped into the corn.
It is later than you think, there is a voice
Preparing to speak, there are whisperings now
And murmuring and noises made with the teeth.
This voice will grow louder and learn a language.
They shall sit trembling while its will is made known,
In gongs struck, bonfires, and shadows on sundials.
Once it has spoken it shall never be silenced.

CLIMBING MILESTONE MOUNTAIN, AUGUST 22, 1937

For a month now, wandering over the Sierras,
A poem had been gathering in my mind,
Details of significance and rhythm,
The way poems do, but still lacking a focus.
Last night I remembered the date and it all
Began to grow together and take on purpose.
 We sat up late while Deneb moved over the zenith
And I told Marie all about Boston, how it looked
That last terrible week, how hundreds stood weeping
Impotent in the streets that last midnight.
I told her how those hours changed the lives of thousands,
How America was forever a different place
Afterwards for many.
                            In the morning
We swam in the cold transparent lake, the blue
Damsel flies on all the reeds like millions
Of narrow metallic flowers, and I thought
Of you behind the grille in Dedham, Vanzetti,
Saying, "Who would ever have thought we would make this
        history?"
Crossing the brilliant mile-square meadow
Illuminated with asters and cyclamen,
The pollen of the lodgepole pines drifting
With the shifting wind over it and the blue
And sulphur butterflies drifting with the wind,
I saw you in the sour prison light, saying,
"Goodbye comrade."
                            In the basin under the crest
Where the pines end and the Sierra primrose begins,
A party of lawyers was shooting at a whiskey bottle.
The bottle stayed on its rock, nobody could hit it.
Looking back over the peaks and canyons from the last lake,
The pattern of human beings seemed simpler
Than the diagonals of water and stone.
Climbing the chute, up the melting snow and broken rock,

I remembered what you said about Sacco,
How it slipped your mind and you demanded it be read
    into the record.
Traversing below the ragged arête,
One cheek pressed against the rock
The wind slapping the other,
I saw you both marching in an army
You with the red and black flag, Sacco with the rattlesnake
    banner.
I kicked steps up the last snow bank and came
To the indescribably blue and fragrant
Polemonium and the dead sky and the sterile
Crystalline granite and final monolith of the summit.
These are the things that will last a long time, Vanzetti,
I am glad that once on your day I have stood among them.
Some day mountains will be named after you and Sacco.
They will be here and your name with them,
"When these days are but a dim remembering of the time
When man was wolf to man."
I think men will be remembering you a long time
Standing on the mountains
Many men, a long time, comrade.

THE NEW YEAR

for Helen

I walk on the cold mountain above the city
Through the black eucalyptus plantation.
Only a few of the million lights
Penetrate the leaves and the dripping fog.
I remember the wintry stars
In the bare branches of the maples,
In the branches of the chestnuts that are gone.

A VERY EARLY MORNING EXERCISE

Chang Yuen is on the threshold of a remarkable career.
He is a minor official in Nanking;
However he is intimate with the highest circles in the
    capital.
Great things are predicted for him;
But he has literary tastes.
He works listlessly and stays up all night;
He wishes times were quieter;
He wishes he could become a monk;
He longs for what he calls social cohesion;
He wishes he lived in a more positive culture.
Anonymously he has published a learned paper,
"On the Precision of Shinto as an Agnostic Cultural
    Determinant."
At times he believes the world is on the verge
Of a Great Spiritual Rebirth.
He is very fond of Rimbaud, Bertrand Russell and Tu Fu.
He wishes he could live in Paris.

He crosses the bridge by the Heavenly Inspiration Textile
    Works.
The long building quivers all over with the rattle of machinery.
In the windows the greenish lights
Wink as the people pass before them.
Porters plunge in and out of vast faint doorways.
Against the fence faces gleam in a heap of rags.
Chang Yuen pauses on the bridge muttering,
"The concubines of the Above One
Dance in transparent gossamer
In the evening at the Purple Phoenix Pavilion."
He thinks of the girls he could have bought for ten dollars
In Shantung during the famine.
He says aloud softly,
"Il faisait chaud, dans la vallée
Bien que le soleil se fût couché depuis longtemps,"
He thinks of the son of his very important friend Won;

He is fourteen years old and goes out at night in Shanghai,
With rouged cheeks in the streets of the International
    Settlement.
He decides to take his opium more seriously.
Pear blossoms fall in the fog,
The tide stirs in the river,
The first dawn glows at the end of the streets.

ANOTHER EARLY MORNING EXERCISE

One hundred feet overhead the fog from the Pacific
Moves swiftly over the hills and houses of San Francisco.
After the bright March day the interior valleys
Suck great quantities of cool air in from the ocean.
Above the torn fog one high, laminated, transparent cloud
Travels slowly northward across the lower half of the
    half-moon.
The moon falls westward in a parabola from Castor and
    Pollux.
I walk along the street at three in the morning,
It is spring in the last year of youth.
The tide is out and the air is full of the smell of the ocean.
The newly arrived mocking birds are awake
In the courtyard behind the houses.
I pass a frosted refrigerated window
Where five disemboweled white hares
Hang by their furred hind paws from a five-spoked rack.
The unlit florists' windows are full of obscure almond
    blossoms.
I have been sitting in Sam Wo's drinking cold aromatic
    liquor.
"What did Borodin do in Canton in 1927" —
The argument lasted five hours.
My friend Soo sympathizes with the Left Opposition;
He told me I had murdered forty thousand bodies on
    Yellow Flower Hill.

"Those bodies are on your shoulders," he said.
He ordered stewed tripe and wept eating it,
Clicking his chopsticks like castanets.
Whatever Borodin did it was probably wrong;
History would be so much simpler if you could just write it
Without ever having to let it happen.
The armies of the Kuo Min Tang have taken the birthplace
    of Tu Fu;
The Red Army has retreated in perfect order.
I wonder if the wooden image erected by his family
Still stands in the shrine at Cheng Tu;
I wonder if any one still burns paper
Before that face of hungry intelligence and sympathy.
He had a hard life he hated war and despotism and famine;
The first chance he got he quarreled with the Emperor.
Venomous papers dry their ink on the newsstands;
A chill comes over me; I walk along shivering;
Thinking of a world full of miserable lives,
And all the men who have been tortured
Because they believed it was possible to be happy.
Pickets keep watch by the bridge over the mouth of the
    Sacramento,
Huddled over small fires,
Talking little,
Rifles in their hands.

AUTUMN IN CALIFORNIA

Autumn in California is a mild
And anonymous season, hills and valleys
Are colorless then, only the sooty green
Eucalyptus, the conifers and oaks sink deep
Into the haze; the fields are plowed, bare, waiting;
The steep pastures are tracked deep by the cattle;
There are no flowers, the herbage is brittle.

All night along the coast and the mountain crests
Birds go by, murmurous, high in the warm air.
Only in the mountain meadows the aspens
Glitter like goldfish moving up swift water;
Only in the desert villages the leaves
Of the cottonwoods descend in smoky air.
  Once more I wander in the warm evening
Calling the heart to order and the stiff brain
To passion. I should be thinking of dreaming, loving, dying,
Beauty wasting through time like draining blood,
And me alone in all the world with pictures
Of pretty women and the constellations.
But I hear the clocks in Barcelona strike at dawn
And the whistles blowing for noon in Nanking.
I hear the drone, the snapping high in the air
Of planes fighting, the deep reverberant
Grunts of bombardment, the hasty clamor
Of anti-aircraft.
                        In Nanking at the first bomb,
A moon-faced, willowy young girl runs into the street,
Leaves her rice bowl spilled and her children crying,
And stands stiff, cursing quietly, her face raised to the sky.
Suddenly she bursts like a bag of water,
And then as the blossom of smoke and dust diffuses,
The walls topple slowly over her.
                        I hear the voices
Young, fatigued and excited, of two comrades
In a closed room in Madrid. They have been up
All night, talking of trout in the Pyrenees,
Spinoza, old nights full of riot and sherry,
Women they might have had or almost had,
Picasso, Velasquez, relativity.
The candlelight reddens, blue bars appear
In the cracks of the shutters, the bombardment
Begins again as though it had never stopped,
The morning wind is cold and dusty,
Their furloughs are over. They are shock troopers,
They may not meet again. The dead light holds

In impersonal focus the patched uniforms,
The dog-eared copy of Lenin's Imperialism,
The heavy cartridge belt, holster and black revolver butt.
    The moon rises late over Mt. Diablo,
Huge, gibbous, warm; the wind goes out,
Brown fog spreads over the bay from the marshes,
And overhead the cry of birds is suddenly
Loud, wiry, and tremulous.

NEW OBJECTIVES, NEW CADRES

Before the inevitable act,
The necessity of decision,
The pauper broken in the ditch,
The politician embarrassed in the council,
Before the secret connivance,
Before the plausible public appearance,
What are the consequences of this adultery?
Ends are not consequences,
Enthusiasm is not integrity,
Hope is not knowledge.
Implements can turn into products,
Concessions into purposes.
By what order must the will walk impugned,
Through spangles of landscape,
Through umbers of sea bottom,
By the casein gleam of any moon
Of postulates and wishes?
Our objectives are not our confidantes,
We cannot retire to the past or the future
Like Franz Josef to his hassenpfeffer mistress.
We found that out.
Who so chooses may look at history
As a plumed courtier gracefully

Bowing himself backwards out of a window.
The treads of the tanks bang on the cobblestones,
The famous Jewish comedian is castrated in an alley,
The coalition cabinet is apprehended at the border,
The minister for foreign affairs commits suicide.
Grown for fear and fattened into groaning
The clawed eyelid or the crushed flower stalk,
Or the undeviating lockstep
The inert incurious onanist,
The rubicund practical prankster,
We wake never in this dispensation
For them or their inchoate brethren,
We watch imaginary just men
Nude as rose petals, discussing a purer logic
In bright functionalist future gymnasia
High in the snows of Mt. Lenin
Beside a collectivist ocean.
But see around the corner in bare lamplight,
In a desquamate basement bedroom,
He who sits in his socks reading shockers,
Skinning cigarette butts and rerolling them in toilet paper,
His red eyes never leaving the blotted print and the pulp paper.
He rose too late to distribute the leaflets.
In the midst of the mussed bedding have mercy
Upon him, this is history.
Or see the arch dialectic satyriast;
Miners' wives and social workers
Rapt in a bated circle about him;
Drawing pointless incisive diagrams
On a blackboard, barking
Ominously with a winey timbre,
Clarifying constant and variable capital,
His subconscious painfully threading its way
Through future slippery assignations.
We do not need his confessions.
The future is more fecund than Molly Bloom—
The problem is to control history,
We already understand it.

AUGUST 22, 1939

"... when you want to distract your mother from the discouraging soulness, I will tell you what I used to do. To take her for a long walk in the quiet country, gathering wildflowers here and there, resting under the shade of trees, between the harmony of the vivid stream and the tranquillity of the mother-nature, and I am sure she will enjoy this very much, as you surely will be happy for it. But remember always, Dante, in the play of happiness, don't use all for yourself only, but down yourself just one step, at your side and help the weak ones that cry for help, help the prosecuted and the victim; because they are your friends; they are the comrades that fight and fall as your father and Bartolo fought and fell yesterday, for the conquest of the joy of freedom for all and the poor workers. In this struggle of life you will find more love and you will be loved."

Nicola Sacco to his son Dante, Aug. 18, 1927.

Angst und Gestalt und Gebet — Rilke

What is it all for, this poetry,
This bundle of accomplishment
Put together with so much pain?
Twenty years at hard labor,
Lessons learned from Li Po and Dante,
Indian chants and gestalt psychology;
What words can it spell,
This alphabet of one sensibility?
The pure pattern of the stars in orderly progression,
The thin air of fourteen-thousand-foot summits,
Their Pisgah views into what secrets of the personality,
The fire of poppies in eroded fields,
The sleep of lynxes in the noonday forest,
The curious anastomosis of the webs of thought,
Life streaming ungovernably away,
And the deep hope of man.
The centuries have changed little in this art,
The subjects are still the same.
"For Christ's sake take off your clothes and get into bed,
We are not going to live forever."
"Petals fall from the rose,"

We fall from life,
Values fall from history like men from shellfire,
Only a minimum survives,
Only an unknown achievement.
They can put it all on the headstones,
In all the battlefields,
"Poor guy, he never knew what it was all about."
Spectacled men will come with shovels in a thousand years,
Give lectures in universities on cultural advances, cultural lags.
A little more garlic in the soup,
A half-hour more in bed in the morning,
Some of them got it, some of them didn't;
The things they dropped in their hurry
Are behind the glass cases of dusky museums.
This year we made four major ascents,
Camped for two weeks at timberline,
Watched Mars swim close to the earth,
Watched the black aurora of war
Spread over the sky of a decayed civilization.
These are the last terrible years of authority.
The disease has reached its crisis,
Ten thousand years of power,
The struggle of two laws,
The rule of iron and spilled blood,
The abiding solidarity of living blood and brain.
They are trapped, beleaguered, murderous,
If they line their cellars with cork
It is not to still the pistol shots,
It is to insulate the last words of the condemned.
"Liberty is the mother
Not the daughter of order."
"Not the government of men
But the administration of things."
"From each according to his ability,
Unto each according to his needs."
We could still hear them,
Cutting steps in the blue ice of hanging glaciers,
Teetering along shattered arêtes.

The cold and cruel apathy of mountains
Has been subdued with a few strands of rope
And some flimsy iceaxes,
There are only a few peaks left.
Twenty-five years have gone since my first sweetheart.
Back from the mountains there is a letter waiting for me.
"I read your poem in the New Republic.
Do you remember the undertaker's on the corner,
How we peeped in the basement window at a sheeted figure
And ran away screaming? Do you remember?
There is a filling station on the corner,
A parking lot where your house used to be,
Only ours and two other houses are left.
We stick it out in the noise and carbon monoxide."
It was a poem of homesickness and exile,
Twenty-five years wandering around
In a world of noise and poison.
She stuck it out, I never went back,
But there are domestic as well as imported
Explosions and poison gases.
Dante was homesick, the Chinese made an art of it,
So was Ovid and many others,
Pound and Eliot amongst them,
Kropotkin dying of hunger,
Berkman by his own hand,
Fanny Baron biting her executioners,
Mahkno in the odor of calumny,
Trotsky, too, I suppose, passionately, after his fashion.
Do you remember?
What is it all for, this poetry,
This bundle of accomplishment
Put together with so much pain?
Do you remember the corpse in the basement?
What are we doing at the turn of our years,
Writers and readers of the liberal weeklies?

NORTH PALISADE,
THE END OF SEPTEMBER, 1939

The sun drops daily down the sky,
The long cold crawls near,
The aspen spills its gold in the air,
Lavish beyond the mind.
This is the last peak, the last climb.
New snow freckles the granite.
The imperious seasons have granted
Courage of a different kind.
Once more only in the smother
Of storm will the wary rope
Vanquish uncertain routes,
This year or another.
Once more only will the peak rise
Lucent above the dropping storm,
Skilled hand and steadfast foot accord
Victory of the brain and eye.
Practice is done, the barren lake
That mirrors this night's fire
Will hold unwinking unknown stars
In its unblemished gaze.

"Now winter nights enlarge
The number of our hours,"
They march to test their power,
We to betray their march.
Their rabbit words and weasel minds
Play at a losing game.
Ours is the unity of aim,
Theirs the diversity of pride.
Their victories on either side
Drive more deep the iron.
Ours is the victory to claim,
Ours is the peace to find.

TOWARD AN ORGANIC PHILOSOPHY

The glow of my campfire is dark red and flameless,
The circle of white ash widens around it.
I get up and walk off in the moonlight and each time
I look back the red is deeper and the light smaller.
Scorpio rises late with Mars caught in his claw;
The moon has come before them, the light
Like a choir of children in the young laurel trees.
It is April; the shad, the hot headed fish,
Climbs the rivers; there is trillium in the damp canyons;
The foetid adder's tongue lolls by the waterfall.
There was a farm at this campsite once, it is almost gone now.
There were sheep here after the farm, and fire
Long ago burned the redwoods out of the gulch,
The Douglas fir off the ridge; today the soil
Is stony and incoherent, the small stones lie flat
And plate the surface like scales.
Twenty years ago the spreading gully
Toppled the big oak over onto the house.
Now there is nothing left but the foundations
Hidden in poison oak, and above on the ridge,
Six lonely, ominous fenceposts;
The redwood beams of the barn make a footbridge
Over the deep waterless creek bed;
The hills are covered with wild oats
Dry and white by midsummer.
I walk in the random survivals of the orchard.
In a patch of moonlight a mole
Shakes his tunnel like an angry vein;
Orion walks waist deep in the fog coming in from the ocean;
Leo crouches under the zenith.
There are tiny hard fruits already on the plum trees.
The purity of the apple blossoms is incredible.
As the wind dies down their fragrance
Clusters around them like thick smoke.
All the day they roared with bees, in the moonlight
They are silent and immaculate.

Once more golden Scorpio glows over the col
Above Deadman Canyon, orderly and brilliant,
Like an inspiration in the brain of Archimedes.
I have seen its light over the warm sea,
Over the coconut beaches, phosphorescent and pulsing;
And the living light in the water
Shivering away from the swimming hand,
Creeping against the lips, filling the floating hair.
Here where the glaciers have been and the snow stays late,
The stone is clean as light, the light steady as stone.
The relationship of stone, ice and stars is systematic and enduring:
Novelty emerges after centuries, a rock spalls from the cliffs,
The glacier contracts and turns grayer,
The stream cuts new sinuosities in the meadow,
The sun moves through space and the earth with it,
The stars change places.
              The snow has lasted longer this year,
Than anyone can remember. The lowest meadow is a lake,
The next two are snowfields, the pass is covered with snow,
Only the steepest rocks are bare. Between the pass
And the last meadow the snowfield gapes for a hundred feet,
In a narrow blue chasm through which a waterfall drops,
Spangled with sunset at the top, black and muscular
Where it disappears again in the snow.
The world is filled with hidden running water
That pounds in the ears like ether;
The granite needles rise from the snow, pale as steel;
Above the copper mine the cliff is blood red,
The white snow breaks at the edge of it;
The sky comes close to my eyes like the blue eyes
Of someone kissed in sleep.
              I descend to camp,
To the young, sticky, wrinkled aspen leaves,
To the first violets and wild cyclamen,
And cook supper in the blue twilight.
All night deer pass over the snow on sharp hooves,
In the darkness their cold muzzles find the new grass
At the edge of the snow.

FALL, SIERRA NEVADA

This morning the hermit thrush was absent at breakfast,
His place was taken by a family of chickadees;
At noon a flock of humming birds passed south,
Whirling in the wind up over the saddle between
Ritter and Banner, following the migration lane
Of the Sierra crest southward to Guatemala.
All day cloud shadows have moved over the face of the mountain,
The shadow of a golden eagle weaving between them
Over the face of the glacier.
At sunset the half-moon rides on the bent back of the Scorpion,
The Great Bear kneels on the mountain.
Ten degrees below the moon
Venus sets in the haze arising from the Great Valley.
Jupiter, in opposition to the sun, rises in the alpenglow
Between the burnt peaks. The ventriloquial belling
Of an owl mingles with the bells of the waterfall.
Now there is distant thunder on the east wind.
The east face of the mountain above me
Is lit with far off lightnings and the sky
Above the pass blazes momentarily like an aurora.
It is storming in the White Mountains,
On the arid fourteen-thousand-foot peaks;
Rain is falling on the narrow gray ranges
And dark sedge meadows and white salt flats of Nevada.
Just before moonset a small dense cumulus cloud,
Gleaming like a grape cluster of metal,
Moves over the Sierra crest and grows down the westward
    slope.
Frost, the color and quality of the cloud,
Lies over all the marsh below my campsite.
The wiry clumps of dwarfed whitebark pines
Are smoky and indistinct in the moonlight,
Only their shadows are really visible.
The lake is immobile and holds the stars
And the peaks deep in itself without a quiver.
In the shallows the geometrical tendrils of ice
Spread their wonderful mathematics in silence.
All night the eyes of deer shine for an instant

As they cross the radius of my firelight.
In the morning the trail will look like a sheep driveway,
All the tracks will point down to the lower canyon.
"Thus," says Tyndall, "the concerns of this little place
Are changed and fashioned by the obliquity of the earth's
    axis,
The chain of dependence which runs through creation,
And links the roll of a planet alike with the interests
Of marmots and of men."

A LETTER TO YVOR WINTERS

Again tonight I read "Before Disaster,"
The tense memento of a will
That's striven thirty years to master
One chaos with one spirit's skill.

As usual, disaster has returned.
Its public and its private round
Are narrow enough—we will have learned
Them quite by heart before we're underground.

Tonight Orion walks above my head
While I pace out my human mile;
At noon the same immeasurable tread
Will move toward Atlas from the Nile.

He too returns upon his ordered path,
While change seeps through his interstellar veins—
The Bull before him in immobile wrath,
The sword and cloud of light against his reins.

These thin imagos that abide decay,
The minds of Winters, Rexroth, and their like,
To fight these senile beasts what else have they
Than "clouds of unknowing,"
                                    Swords that shall not strike?

AN EQUATION FOR MARIE

This dream prorogued
Is not a cause
Is uncaused
And has no seeming

This cause dreams
Of no forlorn notion
Walks
In no dreaming

These eyes seek
Sources in speaking
Lips terminating
In not speaking

This hair suspends
In its atmosphere
Fire particles and sparks
Of wishing truly

This body traverses
Hyperbolas of seeing
Recurs on a conchoid
Another bending above it

If this is waking
In a mode of dreaming
In a mode of causing
Without preceding

For it is being
And no seeming

SONGS FOR MARIE'S LUTEBOOK

1

The blue-eyed grass is opening now,
    Careless of frost,
Out with the first spring wind to blow,
    Careless of cost.

If we could act with such sublime
    Careless confidence,
We might not find with passing time,
    Careless indifference.

2

The sea is quiet, the wind gives over,
    The still heat descends,
Deer drowse in the chamisal cover,
    Where the land ends.

Close to each other on the last crest
    We lie stretched prone,
Watching the sun carry slowly west
    The immense noon.

The day with imperceptible motion
    Declines its light,
Until on Atlantic shores of ocean,
    Steps the night.

Suddenly we know daylight slipping
    Between the trees
And feel bright dawn awake the sleeping
    Antipodes.

3

From the plum the petals blow,
    Powdering your bright hair.
You mourn that they go—
    They sift through windy air.

All your grief won't bring them back,
    Another year they've gone.
Now the myriad leafbuds crack,
    The purple fruit comes on.

4

What years are these that warm your breast,
Their clear flames in your eyes and hair,
That you in their jeweled hours are dressed
So fair and debonaire?

Do you forget that this apparel
You shall not always own?
Time counts the coin you so imperil,
At last calls home his loan.

Shall we youth's wage in wrangling waste
And turn his trade amiss,
And when it is too late for haste,
Remember this?

(Tune: *Greensleeves*)

GIC TO HAR

It is late at night, cold and damp
The air is filled with tobacco smoke.
My brain is worried and tired.
I pick up the encyclopedia,
The volume GIC to HAR,
It seems I have read everything in it,
So many other nights like this.
I sit staring empty-headed at the article Grosbeak,
Listening to the long rattle and pound
Of freight cars and switch engines in the distance.
Suddenly I remember
Coming home from swimming
In Ten Mile Creek,
Over the long moraine in the early summer evening,
My hair wet, smelling of waterweeds and mud.
I remember a sycamore in front of a ruined farmhouse,
And instantly and clearly the revelation
Of a song of incredible purity and joy,
My first rose-breasted grosbeak,
Facing the low sun, his body
Suffused with light.
I was motionless and cold in the hot evening
Until he flew away, and I went on knowing
In my twelfth year one of the great things
Of my life had happened.
Thirty factories empty their refuse in the creek.
The farm has given way to an impoverished suburb
On the parched lawns are starlings, alien and aggressive.
And I am on the other side of the continent
Ten years in an unfriendly city.

FALLING LEAVES AND EARLY SNOW

In the years to come they will say,
"They fell like the leaves
In the autumn of nineteen thirty-nine."
November has come to the forest,
To the meadows where we picked the cyclamen.
The year fades with the white frost
On the brown sedge in the hazy meadows,
Where the deer tracks were black in the morning.
Ice forms in the shadows;
Disheveled maples hang over the water;
Deep gold sunlight glistens on the shrunken stream.
Somnolent trout move through pillars of brown and gold.
The yellow maple leaves eddy above them,
The glittering leaves of the cottonwood,
The olive, velvety alder leaves,
The scarlet dogwood leaves,
Most poignant of all.

In the afternoon thin blades of cloud
Move over the mountains;
The storm clouds follow them;
Fine rain falls without wind.
The forest is filled with wet, resonant silence.
When the rain pauses the clouds
Cling to the cliffs and the waterfalls.
In the evening the wind changes;
Snow falls in the sunset.
We stand in the snowy twilight
And watch the moon rise in a breach of cloud.
Between the black pines lie narrow bands of moonlight,
Glimmering with floating snow.
An owl cries in the sifting darkness.
The moon has a sheen like a glacier.

THE APPLE GARTHS OF AVALON

for the author of the Realms of Being,
both as greeting and as farewell.

Here the face turns
East, wisdom an unwilling
Forced acquisition, turning,
Turns west; the far retinas enfold
Oriented corridors of an ontology
Of mountain fog and cloud and snow
Fed pool of unspecked depth. The turning
Face flushes from the welding point
Bubble of a sun in stone
Sea. He,
Chaperon of a neural frazzle, frayed
In a confusion of multiple demands,
Finds, bright in native reflex,
Awareness tired with waiting; saying,
"Wisdom has been wished
On us. We who wrought an accurate
Exhaustive positivism, having
Constructed a submarine apparatus
Of unique causation, arise
To an unexpected traumatic
Pacific shallow."

These things,
Like fruit dropped in crystal
Water off coral beaches, stand
Alone, remote and warm. The luscious
Fruit of this seized surety attracts
And holds him, Sebastian, electric
In its daedal realm. The dropped
Brittle bubbles rise, minute and myriad,
Off fecund contours; and green,
Blue, and blue green, and fainter
Purple strata quiver,
Flash, and penetrate the eye. Thought,
Transmuted in this polyphony,

Peers the sea reaches; the edge
Of cognition wavers; the inviolate,
Skeptical architecture shatters
About him. Sebastian
Parts lips cauterized
By hypnosis in a world drawn
Suddenly closer to the sun.
Reintegrated, strives for swift
Articulation that shall be
Consonant to this scholia of a chaos made
Perfect and rhythmic and entire.

The epochal purity arriving
Out of condensation and rarefaction,
The ingenerable
In its generation proffering
In a realm, the conquest of caustic
Focus, the ascetic mode
Of apprehension, saying,
"Out of this, once known as death, we pluck
This thistle, life, elicited
After painful labor in the discreet.
We who murdered to dissect, penitent,
Come sentient at this time, in its way
An end, to tactile convictions in edges, blooms
And wavers, the lissome, infinite contingency."

A world of risibles, a world of teems
Of plums, of carrots, and the clotted creams
Of pieced acreages of pale frail greens—
The carbon crystal loam that busts
With cabbage laughter and spinach dreams,
Explodes its fronded fireworks
Out of the belly's wine,
And all the cervine maidens wince away.
The brown road winds down between
The yellow hills and the red trees; the hound
Runs rabbits in the stubble fields and cracks
A million barks against the frosty sun;

And Otto turns the squashes one by one,
His pipe emitting rare fat thistledowns,
Ascending in the autumn clarity.
Ladies your pointed eyes and toes
Curl as last night's leaves uncurl.
The coiffeur curls up and dyes the sculptor he . . .
. . . ah, plummets of abundance fall light years
Through glassy air to burst upon the earth.

(The difference between a coiffeur and a sculptor is that the
coiffeur curls up and dyes, while the sculptor makes faces
and busts.)

THE HEART UNBROKEN AND THE COURAGE FREE

It is late autumn, the end of Indian summer.
It was dry and warm all day, tonight it is cold.
In the light of the quarter moon the hoarfrost
Glows dimly on the dry long grass. A breeze starts
And stops and starts and makes waves on the hillside.
At the edge of the wild raspberry bushes
Four sooty spots bob about against the white frost.
They are rabbits with cold noses and cold toes.
Castor and Pollux blur in the first edge of fog.
Your breath is visible like fine autumn down,
Your eyes are polished with moonlight,
I look at them, they are the color of snow.

ORGANON

1

Intact as concave
For cause as varnished
Marginal dreamed and finally
Insistent the thick
Leaf or morning dim
And expanding in the
Piece and cave the
Breaking shell in
The fist or the adhesion of the living
Hand the wall paused and
Preserved so spoken the question
Perduring therefore in
Living thought may risk
Assault of what selection
Surprises the total
Of temptations and disasters
Slow
Credentials of catastrophe
The flamboyant
Awaiting in the
Occurring over no
Theft of sign no
Inch of air
Elude
For
He who expected the endurance avoided the concomitants
Others seeking
Elsewhere
Thick leaf and slope
Of loess
And harsh
Leather and eyeball
Of dyed sandstone
Squat foetid men in the dim
Room and the living

Bone strode in air the living
On the ground the book
Cut with knives
With morning
And interrogation
The preserved confused
Reality
Intact
Tactile

2

Lost in white of an implacable
Unity, disguised and separate,
The emergent is not thus present
To question or even thus present
For fact. For fact, tangled in solvents
Of disintegrate and partial shock,
Is pain and pain alone, is never
Quick cause nor parent nor child thereof.
Who is this who surprises coffins
In the sky early in the morning,
Whose eyes were welded in the desert?
Not a dream but a knife, neither peace,
But many small live bombs like maggots,
Squirming in the shadow of cactus,
Replace the micrometers, the hands
Of distinctions; and the living spleen,
Moving spongewise across the ceiling
Of the liver, now painstakingly
Erases the auguries bitten by process,
Obliterates the spoor
Of razors and of sleep; now ether
Rains from the stone, hastily ignites;
And the bombs speak like small birds chirping—
And the little iota, the thing
That caused so much worry to so few,
Spinning like burning paper in wind,
Passes beyond the range of vision.

3

The minutes of the tongue are gone in,
And the volumes are closed behind them,
The small prisms and large ellipsoids,
The peppers withering in the heat.
Being accumulates negatives
Thus, electrolyzed, indifferent,
Hoarding deprivation as passage
Through entity of luminous flux
Of zeros exploding asymptotes
Hands Lips Fingers Mallets Tapers Orbs
The insect agile in utter sky,
Omnivorous, constructed, intact,
And the petals crawling, and the heat,
And the falling copper and the felt stone.

4

As fact wastes out of experience
Leaving no promise of conservation
Or perpetuity of those ultimates
Deposited in the experient,
And deaths and negatives waste being;
The erosion of being to what is,
Elimination in logic, and passage
Of history, effective equally—
And only values prime and promised
Surviving, and only dubiously—
Being as vital becomes a postulant
Of hope, a struggle of *sein* and *sosein*,
Whose only assurance is moral.

Distinction implies difference: awaited
Predicate and cleft particular
As a demonstrable otherness, as fact
And factual presuppose in act,
An act, comparison, configuration—
Always constitutive, primitive
And elicited first for presentation

As assertable pattern, precise,
Intransitive, adjective, impersonal;
Or difference implies distinction
As being imperative separateness
Of epistemic material,
Imperative enumerability
For proposition and decision.

It is a wise one in the early morning
Met in two halves and a wise
Standing as a thing act being
Gracious or divisible the
Opposition standing the
Channels cross and return this being
This instant thing and small as
Verb affect going a minute
Verb green to a hooded term
Shape part one and go back
Go back a gentle being
Being and gone to a meant term
Doing this is the stop
But wait but wait a box
Wait a bar going and a place
For the white meters crossing
The plug makes the glass hand
Square or once squared and the crossed
Metric going being
Falling

If difference is a being thing
And a pointing raises moving
Or stops break and dry
So instant make or growing
So meaning asking
And shall have been in cause
Risen is a mark or two no a
Question as is thing and
Removal desire not divide

116

Volume not the preceding
And weight not value
For pain and parts
Risen saying going
Moves doubted or off
Small one careful
Whereupon a way
Lift
Know
Pass

If in the imagined case it can
Be or is less than it is or there
Are two rights to the number
The chance speaking wages position
And the effort is going effort
In the way the travel out
Knows shape and the in mover
Forms then possible as thought
Opens as petals and close
Darkens large as dim long
Gathers or force a granted
To wing motion this is a less
Instant and the dividing
A mode happen in tight
And a place place
To speak it was there
A single old

DATIVE HARUSPICES

Film and filament, no
Donor, gift without
Reciprocity, transparent
Tactile act, an imaginary
Web of structure sweeps
The periphery of being, glass
Entities point, the fundamental
Entails arise, ominous
Real, augurs move in sleep
Voices break the vast
Indifferent sarcophagus, this
Source and word, secret, never
Fractured by volition
Seventy years
Hidden, the hangman
In the navel, or
An eye in the oblivion
Of an instantaneous
Being of a differential
Flexible beyond assent
Sentient webs morseled with fact
Parcel now in the sky, compact
Parabolas branch in a capsule
Punctured with instants, ominous of items
Stars Palps Needles
Where the central summation extrudes
Inhibited muscular tensors, what
Recall of pentacles, bulbs
Uttered in scissors loan, are being
Is sown on the rent
Tumuli, what ing in the ever
Lasting (there are no horizons
In mountains, but
Dispersed minutes itemize the skyline, stones
Are accepted by canyons with uniform

Acceleration and snow
Disturbed by wind hovers in sun
Light in the passes) directrices
Of becoming, courteous
In the differentials
With what fact
For an endless time being
Watching luminous songs utter
The round earth visible
As the moon moves
Men move from a distance
Men sleep overhead
A word a fire
Occurs endures for
Generations a slow body
Swings in space warm
Water pulled by the moon
Fog descends on the nostrils
Having died in its
Heart what pulse will
Ripen planes lift in dark
And move mice sleep
A sloth moves head down
The child sleeps
Guarded by an arrow
In what hour

VALUE IN MOUNTAINS

1

There are those to whom value is a weapon,
Collectors of negatives and ascertables,
And those to whom value is horror,
Themselves collected by evaluation;
Who, recurrently dispossessed in each judgment,
Seizing or seized by presented fact,
Explode in a fury of discreet instants.
    Being is social in its immediacy,
Private in final implications;
Life is built of contact and dies secretly;
So existants live in history and die out
In fulfillment of individuals.
    Thus value is a food and not a weapon
Nor a challenge, process, not result, of judgment,
The morituri te salutamus
Of unique atomic realizations,
Enduring only in their eschatologies.

2

The shields of the peltasts of
The imagination quiver in the
Imagination the flourish
Of fire curves on the border
The eyelids gold and blue
The place of penumbras
Iris and pupil
Frosted or a star
Falling past Deneb
Past Aldebaran
Falling all night
Heavy as the songs
Arhythmic atonal
That drift with smoke
Across water

Or the cry rising
From between the buttes
The myrmidons
Of the imagination emerge
From stones
And sleep

3

Peace above this arch urged and bent, rising out
The frieze that not till high cold air in that time
Grown earthward vatic, incomprehensible
In trees inverted and copper galls of bloom,
Spoke death as speaking wrought; rhymed the butterflies;
Pared away rinds of thinking finer than thought;
Constructed tissues of a death of moments;
The translucent frieze of petals, of blue leaves,
Opposed blocked men with red granite molar hands;
Opposed the somnolescent will in its fact;
Bespoke the exfoliation of decay;
Compressed the angles at which the rods had leaned;
Stirred in the mind; settled the beams of passage;
Spoke death as fact, as fiat of becoming.
    The three shamen in their castle cubicles
Restored the prisms; replaced the discs and cubes;
Wrenched the taut lines welded in the cone of rays.
    Death spoke in atoms, speaking fine blown parsings
Of collected passage, syntax of the crumb.

4

He strikes the two rocks
He casts the four seeds
He marks in the dust
He draws three triangles
He burns the five feathers
He barks like the coyote
He paints his face white
He runs away

Has the arrow stood erect
The cones falling in cold water
All night the bell
And the delicate feet
A thousand leaves spinning
In the cube of ten thousand leaves
Or the cube that descends like a mist
The speaking voice will issue
From between immaculate red
And white alternates

The immediate fact
Is not perdurable
And speaking is being memory
The prisms falling in snow
Or web of air
And silver target
And the unique
Note
Of the stricken

EASY LESSONS IN GEOPHAGY

for Hart Crane and Harry Crosby

"pulldo pulldo shows quoth the caliver"
Eastward Hoe

1

The Leonids having fallen
The tinkles having fallen
The silver having fallen silently
Having the fog
Having the colorless margin
Having the gold bees
The act having been forgotten
The right hand having turned sinister

Can the indifferent arms be raised
Moving in the tree tops
Sounding the long horn
Seeing the red animals
Floating among the transparent medusae
Canopus hears the moon hears
The night the members
Of the body move in the sea
In the saline transparent sea
Auguries of struggle urge the somatic
Community fluent webs run
Through the viscera the head
Appears in air the nostrils
The eyes open the lips open the whites
Of the eyes shine over
The groundswell the great conch speaks
The knowledge of war spreads over the water
The brittle bones watching
The spider
In a bar of light
In the sound of water

2

"In time all haggard hawks will stoop to lure"
The needle digests the eagle
The tile eyeballs
The painted marbles
The falsetto tornado interrupts itself
With shaved foxhounds
With unworthy insights
With hand-painted paraboloids
With cotton metronomes
With little beetles
The needle digests the eagle
They have programs in going
Away went conquests
Away went nodes and interruptions
Away went unmistakable punctuations

The kite screams and falls screaming
And falls blood streaming from its eyes
And falls its beak shattered
And falls in a tangent to the horizon
And falls whirling
And falls in mixed helices
And falls screaming
And falls into the spinning freezer
The resilient thumb presses the patent mattress
Three glimmers replace the hair
The scalp moves in recurrent conchoids
The undulation digests the albatross
Little cubes
The base whistle continues
Endures like the green hippocephali
Endures like the acknowledged error
Endures like the Gulf of Spoiled Botanies
Endures like the mincer
Endures like the worms of longitude
Ostriches digest needles
The dead are fed to the vultures
And the broken rhythmic vertigo recurs continually

3

"Born into it
Proved by external effects
Proved by internal effects
Thus literally living in a blaze of reality"
Is it fear to meet as he might meet fear
Meeting himself in the burnt forest
Is it fear avoiding the personal
Pronoun avoiding the eponymoi of myself
Amongst the innumerable black infusoria
I come so to the comet traps
I come so to the gegenschein
I come so to the more obscure aurora
I come so to the vital organs

Arranged on a shelf above the body
Guarded by the effigies of their patrons
When they spoke of a man they said you see
That was a different time in another
Place they spoke of another they said instead
Of succulents do you prefer kelp
Or cactus instead
Of the calipers the splintered ice

4

I passed the black fountain
I passed the swathed man
I passed the meteorite
I passed the tireless mice
I passed the long shark of the dawn
I passed the multitude of gelid eardrums
There are no teeth in most orchids
The bas-relief tilts in the wall
Flowers explode beneath the feet of the horses
And the earthquake announces its genesis by whistling in the
    thermometers, and
Announces its approach by obscuring the pulsations of the flowers
The earthquake speaks gently and distinctly in a foreign language.

Born into it
Proved by external effects
Proved by internal effects
Light is reddened by age, it loses energy as it gets older,
    traveling through space.

A LESSON IN GEOGRAPHY

*"of Paradys ne can not I speken
propurly ffor I was not there"*
Mandeville

The stars of the Great Bear drift apart
The Horse and the Rider together northeastward
Alpha and Omega asunder
The others diversely
There are rocks
On the earth more durable
Than the configurations of heaven
Species now motile and sanguine
Shall see the stars in new clusters
The beaches changed
The mountains shifted
Gigantic
Immobile
Floodlit
The faces appear and disappear
Chewing the right gum
Smoking the right cigarette
Buying the best refrigerator
The polished carnivorous teeth
Exhibited in approval
The lights
Of the houses
Draw together
In the evening dewfall on the banks
Of the Wabash
Sparkle discreetly
High on the road to Provo
Above the Salt Lake Valley
And
The mountain shaped like a sphinx
And
The mountain shaped like a finger
Pointing

On the first of April at eight o'clock
Precisely at Algol
There are rocks on the earth
And one who sleepless
Throbbed with the ten
Nightingales in the plum trees
Sleepless as Boötes stood over him
Gnawing the pillow
Sitting on the bed's edge smoking
Sitting by the window looking
One who rose in the false
Dawn and stoned
The nightingales in the garden
The heart pawned for wisdom
The heart
Bartered for knowledge and folly
The will troubled
The mind secretly aghast
The eyes and lips full of sorrow
The apices of vision wavering
As the flower spray at the tip of the windstalk
The becalmed sail
The heavy wordless weight
And now
The anguishing and pitiless file
Cutting away life
Capsule by capsule biting
Into the heart
The coal of fire
Sealing the lips
There are rocks on earth

And

In the Japanese quarter
A phonograph playing
"Moonlight on ruined castles"
Kojo n'suki

And
The movement of the wind fish
Keeping time to the music
Sirius setting behind it
(The Dog has scented the sun)
Gold immense fish
Squirm in the trade wind
"Young Middle Western woman
In rut
Desires correspondent"
The first bright flower
Cynoglossum
The blue hound's tongue
Breaks on the hill
"The tide has gone down
Over the reef
I walk about the world
There is great
Wind and then rain"
"My life is bought and paid for
So much pleasure
For so much pain"
The folded fossiliferous
Sedimentary rocks end here
The granite batholith
Obtrudes abruptly
West of the fault line
Betelgeuse reddens
Drawing its substance about it
It is possible that a process is beginning
Similar to that which lifted
The great Sierra fault block
Through an older metamorphic range

(The Dog barks on the sun's spoor)

Now

The thought of death
Binds fast the flood of light
Ten years ago the snow falling
All a long winter night
I had lain waking in my bed alone
Turning my heavy thoughts
And no way might
Sleep
Remembering divers things long gone
Now
In the long day in the hour of small shadow
I walk on the continent's last western hill
And lie prone among the iris in the grass
My eyes fixed on the durable stone
That speaks and hears as though it were myself

NORTHAMPTON, 1922—
SAN FRANCISCO, 1939

All night rain falls through fog.
I lie awake, restless on a twisted pillow.
Fog horns cry over the desolate water.
How long ago was it,
That night with the pear blossoms
Quivering in the pulsating moonlight?
I am startled from sleep
By the acrid fleshy odor of pear blossoms.

Somewhere in the world, I suppose,
You are still living, a middle-aged matron,
With children on the verge of youth.

ICE SHALL COVER NINEVEH

"But have you heard that, once upon a time, the city of Nineveh stood where now one sees the snow fields of the Gurgler Glacier? I do not know myself whether it is true or not. They say that a pilgrim came there and asked for bread. The people were miserly and gave him only a sour crust. He rebuked them, and after his departure, ice came and covered their city. I have heard that he was one of the Three Wise Men. . . .

"Austrian guns were mounted on the south peak of the Ortler, and all the way down to the Payer hut we shall find the remains of cables up which supplies were carried during the last weeks of conflict. . . .

"Tomorrow when you cross the Stelvio, you will see the galleries and rock-cut trenches where many men lived and died. They were mountain men like those cutting hay in the fields by which we passed. There was no hatred in their hearts. Word came from the cities that they must go out and kill."

"Ice Shall Cover Nineveh"—J. MONROE THORINGTON
Sierra Club Bulletin, 1933

1

Distant on the meridian verges
And the soft equinoxes calling
Altair burns over the glacial
Pyramid it is evening
And the nighthawks pass over me
The great heron lifts from the water
And goes away the evening deepens
The stars come out and the owls under them
Dew falls between the mountains
And the Milky Way
Treeless and desolate
The lake lies under the last mountain
The moon rises and falling
Fringes of storm clouds blow over it
The wind barks in the cleft of the mountain
Sheep bells move in the valleys under me
The owls spiral close to the ground
The rain thickens and they go away
Lightning unwinds over the summit
I turn in sleep and speak aloud

2

Under the surgical and unnoticed
Sun now the gray rare
Condor goes over his swimming
Shadow over the matted alpine
Hemlock and gold trout waltz and
Flash in the volatile water
The mind splinters in attenuate air
The trail curls
Movement whistles into pain
The ache of bone the ache
Of immemorial blood
The sun goes under
The prostrate wood
The stars come over
The standing stone
Sacrifices and populations dissolve
We shall go away and not know when
Awakened at night and far away
In dense valleys bright life needles every clod
Neither fortified in dolmen nor reclined
In tumulus shall white throat and quick hand hide
Nor eye escape the rasp of powdering time

3

We would hear the sheep bells at night
And sometimes by day with the wind changing
But we spent two days hunting and calling
Because the tableland was full of wrinkles
With all sizes of lakes in them and covered
With stones the size and color of sheep
And then coming back from the pass
She saw in the dark his pipe glowing
And there he was standing against a big rock
A shadow on the pale stone watching the moon rise
Nothing would cook in water at that height
We lived for a week on fried fish bacon and flapjacks
Cooked over the cow dung of the herd
That had been through there two years back

4

The donations of this pattern
Intractable fact or hopeful
Platonism await the issue
Of type or archetype
Of being and existence
Desire anxious and faint
With expectation
Where the shrill
Gasp of spume the cord of water
Hangs from the arid granite
In the lacunae
Of space the interstices
Of the brain
Black wing and rose head
The yellow climbing bird
In the blue haze
Singing over the chasm
Or conversely who shall question
The donor who shall accept
With courtesy and illumination
The chill ground light
The clouds still orange and purple the sky
Unfathomed green
And dark cumbrous and busy
The bears in the huckleberries
Dampness rising from the meadow
The broken moon arriving
Ubiquitously through cloven rock
Or who shall sieve history
The adamant occasion
In bright obstinacy
From this obdurate avalanche

5

No ritual nor prayer shall let
Ungrind this molar precision of
Catastrophe nor shall bespeak
The stars of this vacant absolute
Tragedies swarm polarized between

Cerebrum and cerebellum infest
The wainscotting infest the medulla
Infest the endocrines
Light entering your eyes becomes
Brilliant with worms
All through the twilight air
Creeps a fog of nematodes
And no unguent
No moonlight wafer setting
In your final sky shall still
The roar of falling iron and stone
Falling with lightning and indifference
Beyond knowledge
And beyond interruption

6

Discover the apostleship of diffidence
As gently as bubbles circle out from
The foot of this waterfall and the sun
Declines as carefully find out the torc
And tension of this straight evangel as:
"Again they walk with me who once beside
Me walked the careful feet beside me waked
The meadow lark from the starlit white wheat"
(The song countered against a sun of three thousand suns
The inch-long blur of wings the humming bird
Hung in the fecund air) speak to the fractured
Moments of the aspen the military
Precise marsh iris intercolumniate
With fir and hemlock in smoke of twisted juniper
Memory ascends the mind
Goes up
Assents
The moon early after sundown
The emerald
Long mountain meadow
At the far end
Thirty
Red cattle
Below the peaks

7

A white body prone beneath meteors
And no moon in the moist night
Let a note ring in the immobile forest
The warped gong shuddering as the swung beam struck
Across the peaks clouds rise against the snow
The small eyes
Birds' feet
Flies' wings
And all voice still
Only the catheaded bird wavers through the sequoias
Only the bear snuffs shuffling and the marten
Stretches sliteyed on a branch and sleeps
And the bronze body prone all day beneath
The hunting hawks all day soaring
Spirals in the narrow canyon sky
Falling suddenly to the moved grass
The two red-tailed hawks in the evening go off across the
    mountain
Let the gong speak in the impenetrable granite

8

The sudden eyes of gravid mice
The sunset on the blades of stone
The wide glow of a star falling across
Scorpio in the final altitudes
The crisp utterance of Spica in the evening
The light white in the pools water falling
Luminous through the bat quick air
Glory flashes once and is gone and we go
Stumbling but this is a slow omnivorous
Glory and endures as the mind shrivels
And the electric cancer of the eclipse
Crawls into the sky over the snow

9

Fear no more the eye of the sun
Nor the covert lemming's glance
You the invisible medusa
Have seen at twilight
And the waters wash on shell beaches
Pale blue in the long pale days
And the doe and new fawn cross the bars
Of sunlight under the marsh lodgepole pines
Fear no more Polaris' sword
Nor the noiseless water vole
Nor any brilliant invertebrate
Nor molten nematode
Only the inorganic residues
Of your aspiration remain
Combed over by constellations
Vivisected by blades of wind
Fear no more the chill of the moon
No brisk rodent fear
Nor thirty years' dreams of falling
For frozen on the fixed final summit
Your mineral eyes reflect the gleaming
Perpetual fall of a cube of singular stone
Coursing its own parabola
Beyond imagination
Unto ages of ages

10

You return breathless having startled
Phoenixes in the arroyos and seen
On porphyry altars the pelican
Rend itself tirelessly and the creature
With uncounted eyes
And who now creaking in rust soft armor
Will bring this taper to the outer room
O the lost phalanxes the engulfed Gemini
Where the guillotine animal flies over the drowned lands
And the bleached heads turn incuriously

And no hand lifts
This Prometheus breeds his own eaglets
At first daybreak a voice opens crevices in the air
Fear no more
The horns of those gray hunters wind along
Ridges more inaccessible than dreams
Speak not let no word break
The stillness of this anguish
The omniscience of this vertigo
These lucent needles are fluent
In the gold of every memory
The past curls like wire

11

And now surprised by lunar mountain avatars
The avid eyes of gravid mice entice
Each icy nostrum of the zodiac
Sidelong on quavering feet the giants tread
The white Excaliburs the zero saws
The igneous granite pencils silvering
The plunge of light the coneys barking
The white lips speak and Danae
Danae writhing in the fluent metal
The camels the llamas the dogsleds the burros
Are loaded and go off in the white distance
And green over them the nova grows above the pass

12

Shall ask no more then forget the asker
Shall fail at laughter and in the dark
Go mumbling the parched gums fumbling the baggy heart
Bark with the mice in the rubbish bayed at by rats
The glaciers are senile and covered with dust but the mountain cracks
The orange-red granite breaks and the long black slivers fall
Fine ice in the air and the stone blades falling and the opening vault
The high milk-blue lake tipping over its edge in a mile-long wavering waterfall
And for these weapons in what forge and from what steel
And for this wheat what winnowing floor what flail

THE PHOENIX AND THE TORTOISE

(1944)

For Marie

I would not have you less than mutable,
Leaf wickered sunlight on your lips,
And on your lips the plangent, unstable
Laughter of your copious heart.

WHEN WE WITH SAPPHO

"... about the cool water
the wind sounds through sprays
of apple, and from the quivering leaves
slumber pours down ..."

We lie here in the bee filled, ruinous
Orchard of a decayed New England farm,
Summer in our hair, and the smell
Of summer in our twined bodies,
Summer in our mouths, and summer
In the luminous, fragmentary words
Of this dead Greek woman.
Stop reading. Lean back. Give me your mouth.
Your grace is as beautiful as sleep.
You move against me like a wave
That moves in sleep.
Your body spreads across my brain
Like a bird filled summer;
Not like a body, not like a separate thing,
But like a nimbus that hovers
Over every other thing in all the world.
Lean back. You are beautiful,
As beautiful as the folding
Of your hands in sleep.

We have grown old in the afternoon.
Here in our orchard we are as old
As she is now, wherever dissipate
In that distant sea her gleaming dust
Flashes in the wave crest
Or stains the murex shell.
All about us the old farm subsides
Into the honey bearing chaos of high summer.
In those far islands the temples
Have fallen away, and the marble
Is the color of wild honey.
There is nothing left of the gardens

That were once about them, of the fat
Turf marked with cloven hooves.
Only the sea grass struggles
Over the crumbled stone,
Over the splintered steps,
Only the blue and yellow
Of the sea, and the cliffs
Red in the distance across the bay.
Lean back.
Her memory has passed to our lips now.
Our kisses fall through summer's chaos
In our own breasts and thighs.

Gold colossal domes of cumulus cloud
Lift over the undulant, sibilant forest.
The air presses against the earth.
Thunder breaks over the mountains.
Far off, over the Adirondacks,
Lightning quivers, almost invisible
In the bright sky, violet against
The grey, deep shadows of the bellied clouds.
The sweet virile hair of thunder storms
Brushes over the swelling horizon.
Take off your shoes and stockings.
I will kiss your sweet legs and feet
As they lie half buried in the tangle
Of rank scented midsummer flowers.
Take off your clothes. I will press
Your summer honeyed flesh into the hot
Soil, into the crushed, acrid herbage
Of midsummer. Let your body sink
Like honey through the hot
Granular fingers of summer.

Rest. Wait. We have enough for a while.
Kiss me with your mouth
Wet and ragged, your mouth that tastes
Of my own flesh. Read to me again
The twisting music of that language

That is of all others, itself a work of art.
Read again those isolate, poignant words
Saved by ancient grammarians
To illustrate the conjugations
And declensions of the more ancient dead.
Lean back in the curve of my body,
Press your bruised shoulders against
The damp hair of my body.
Kiss me again. Think, sweet linguist,
In this world the ablative is impossible.
No other one will help us here.
We must help ourselves to each other.
The wind walks slowly away from the storm;
Veers on the wooded crests; sounds
In the valleys. Here we are isolate,
One with the other; and beyond
This orchard lies isolation,
The isolation of all the world.
Never let anything intrude
On the isolation of this day,
These words, isolate on dead tongues,
This orchard, hidden from fact and history,
These shadows, blended in the summer light,
Together isolate beyond the world's reciprocity.

Do not talk any more. Do not speak.
Do not break silence until
We are weary of each other.
Let our fingers run like steel
Carving the contours of our bodies' gold.
Do not speak. My face sinks
In the clotted summer of your hair.
The sound of the bees stops.
Stillness falls like a cloud.
Be still. Let your body fall away
Into the awe filled silence
Of the fulfilled summer—
Back, back, infinitely away—
Our lips weak, faint with stillness.

See. The sun has fallen away.
Now there are amber
Long lights on the shattered
Boles of the ancient apple trees.
Our bodies move to each other
As bodies move in sleep;
At once filled and exhausted,
As the summer moves to autumn,
As we, with Sappho, move towards death.
My eyelids sink toward sleep in the hot
Autumn of your uncoiled hair.
Your body moves in my arms
On the verge of sleep;
And it is as though I held
In my arms the bird filled
Evening sky of summer.

RUNAWAY

There are sparkles of rain on the bright
Hair over your forehead;
Your eyes are wet and your lips
Wet and cold, your cheek rigid with cold.
Why have you stayed
Away so long, why have you only
Come to me late at night
After walking for hours in wind and rain?
Take off your dress and stockings;
Sit in the deep chair before the fire.
I will warm your feet in my hands;
I will warm your breasts and thighs with kisses.
I wish I could build a fire
In you that would never go out.
I wish I could be sure that deep in you
Was a magnet to draw you always home.

LUTE MUSIC

The earth will be going on a long time
Before it finally freezes;
Men will be on it; they will take names,
Give their deeds reasons.
We will be here only
As chemical constituents—
A small franchise indeed.
Right now we have lives,
Corpuscles, ambitions, caresses,
Like everybody had once—
All the bright neige d'antan people,
"Blithe Helen, white Iope, and the rest,"
All the uneasy, remembered dead.

Here at the year's end, at the feast
Of birth, let us bring to each other
The gifts brought once west through deserts—
The precious metal of our mingled hair,
The frankincense of enraptured arms and legs,
The myrrh of desperate, invincible kisses—
Let us celebrate the daily
Recurrent nativity of love,
The endless epiphany of our fluent selves,
While the earth rolls away under us
Into unknown snows and summers,
Into untraveled spaces of the stars.

FLOATING

Our canoe idles in the idling current
Of the tree and vine and rush enclosed
Backwater of a torpid midwestern stream;
Revolves slowly, and lodges in the glutted
Waterlilies. We are tired of paddling.
All afternoon we have climbed the weak current,
Up dim meanders, through woods and pastures,
Past muddy fords where the strong smell of cattle
Lay thick across the water; singing the songs
Of perfect, habitual motion; ski songs,
Nightherding songs, songs of the capstan walk,
The levee, and the roll of the voyageurs.
Tired of motion, of the rhythms of motion,
Tired of the sweet play of our interwoven strength,
We lie in each other's arms and let the palps
Of waterlily leaf and petal hold back
All motion in the heat thickened, drowsing air.
Sing to me softly, Westron Wynde, Ah the Syghes,
Mon coeur se recommend à vous, Phoebi Claro;
Sing the wandering erotic melodies
Of men and women gone seven hundred years,
Softly, your mouth close to my cheek.
Let our thighs lie entangled on the cushions,
Let your breasts in their thin cover
Hang pendant against my naked arms and throat;
Let your odorous hair fall across our eyes;
Kiss me with those subtle, melodic lips.
As I undress you, your pupils are black, wet,
Immense, and your skin ivory and humid.
Move softly, move hardly at all, part your thighs,
Take me slowly while our gnawing lips
Fumble against the humming blood in our throats.
Move softly, do not move at all, but hold me,
Deep, still, deep within you, while time slides away,
As this river slides beyond this lily bed,
And the thieving moments fuse and disappear
In our mortal, timeless flesh.

ANOTHER SPRING

The seasons revolve and the years change
With no assistance or supervision.
The moon, without taking thought,
Moves in its cycle, full, crescent, and full.

The white moon enters the heart of the river;
The air is drugged with azalea blossoms;
Deep in the night a pine cone falls;
Our campfire dies out in the empty mountains.

The sharp stars flicker in the tremulous branches;
The lake is black, bottomless in the crystalline night;
High in the sky the Northern Crown
Is cut in half by the dim summit of a snow peak.

O heart, heart, so singularly
Intransigent and corruptible,
Here we lie entranced by the starlit water,
And moments that should each last forever

Slide unconsciously by us like water.

NIGHT BELOW ZERO

3 A.M., the night is absolutely still;
Snow squeals beneath my skis, plumes on the turns.
I stop at the canyon's edge, stand looking out
Over the Great Valley, over the millions—
In bed, drunk, loving, tending mills, furnaces,
Alone, wakeful, as the world rolls in chaos.
The quarter moon rises in the black heavens—
Over the sharp constellations of the cities
The cold lies, crystalline and silent,
Locked between the mountains.

THE ADVANTAGES OF LEARNING

I am a man with no ambitions
And few friends, wholly incapable
Of making a living, growing no
Younger, fugitive from some just doom.
Lonely, ill-clothed, what does it matter?
At midnight I make myself a jug
Of hot white wine and cardamon seeds.
In a torn grey robe and old beret,
I sit in the cold writing poems,
Drawing nudes on the crooked margins,
Copulating with sixteen year old
Nymphomaniacs of my imagination.

HABEAS CORPUS

You have the body, blood and bone,
And hair and nail and tooth and eye.
You have the body—the skin taut
In the moonlight, the sea gnawing
At the empty mountains, the hair
Of the body tensile, erect . . .
The full barley ears whip and flail
In the rain gorged wind and the flame
Of lightning breaks in the air
For a moment and vanishes;
And I tell you the memory
Of flesh is as real as live flesh
Or falling stone or burning fire . . .
You have the body and the sun
Brocaded brown and pink naked
Wedded body, its eternal
Blood biding the worm and his time.

PLINY — IX, XXXVI —
LAMPRIDIUS — XXIX

When I remember that letter of Pliny's—
The daily round of a gentleman
Of letters in the days of Trajan—
Masseuses of assorted colors
Before breakfast, all of them learned
In the Greek poets, philosophic
Discourses in the bath, flute players
For lunch, along with mathematics,
Roast peacocks for dinner, and after,
Mixed maenads, or else astronomy,
Depending on the mood and weather—
I am overcome with amazement.
Here I sit, poor, proud, and domestic,
Manipulating my typewriter;
And beyond my library window,
Inordinately luxuriant,
Suffused with esoteric giggles,
The remote daughters of my neighbors
Return from high school.

HARMODIUS AND ARISTOGEITON

Last night, reading the Anthology,
I could find no epitaph for you.
I suppose it was naive to look.
Alexander and Justinian,
The brocaded Paleologoi,
French drunkards and sleepy Turks,
Have ruled over Athens since your day.
So, late by these many years, take this:

Your act is vocal still. Men grow deaf.

INVERSELY, AS THE SQUARE OF
THEIR DISTANCES APART

It is impossible to see anything
In this dark; but I know this is me, Rexroth,
Plunging through the night on a chilling planet.
It is warm and busy in this vegetable
Darkness where invisible deer feed quietly.
The sky is warm and heavy, even the trees
Over my head cannot be distinguished,
But I know they are knobcone pines, that their cones
Endure unopened on the branches, at last
To grow imbedded in the wood, waiting for fire
To open them and reseed the burned forest.
And I am waiting, alone, in the mountains,
In the forest, in the darkness, and the world
Falls swiftly on its measured ellipse.

It is warm tonight and very still.
The stars are hazy and the river—
Vague and monstrous under the fireflies—
Is hardly audible, resonant
And profound at the edge of hearing.
I can just see your eyes and wet lips.
Invisible, solemn, and fragrant,
Your flesh opens to me in secret.
We shall know no further enigma.
After all the years there is nothing
Stranger than this. We who know ourselves
As one doubled thing, and move our limbs
As deft implements of one fused lust,
Are mysteries in each other's arms.

At the wood's edge in the moonlight
We dropped our clothes and stood naked,
Swaying, shadow mottled, enclosed
In each other and together
Closed in the night. We did not hear
The whip-poor-will, nor the aspen's
Whisper; the owl flew silently
Or cried out loud, we did not know.
We could not hear beyond the heart.
We could not see the moving dark
And light, the stars that stood or moved,
The stars that fell. Did they all fall
We had not known. We were falling
Like meteors, dark through black cold
Toward each other, and then compact,
Blazing through air into the earth.

I lie alone in an alien
Bed in a strange house and morning
More cruel than any midnight
Pours its brightness through the window—
Cherry branches with the flowers
Fading, and behind them the gold
Stately baubles of the maple,
And behind them the pure immense
April sky and a white frayed cloud,
And in and behind everything,
The inescapable vacant
Distance of loneliness.

VITAMINS AND ROUGHAGE

Strong ankled, sun burned, almost naked,
The daughters of California
Educate reluctant humanists;
Drive into their skulls with tennis balls
The unhappy realization
That nature is still stronger than man.
The special Hellenic privilege
Of the special intellect seeps out
At last in this irrigated soil.
Sweat of athletes and juice of lovers
Are stronger than Socrates' hemlock;
And the games of scrupulous Euclid
Vanish in the gymnopaedia.

BETWEEN TWO WARS

Remember that breakfast one November—
Cold black grapes smelling faintly
Of the cork they were packed in,
Hard rolls with hot, white flesh,
And thick, honey sweetened chocolate?
And the parties at night; the gin and the tangos?
The torn hair nets, the lost cuff links?
Where have they all gone to,
The beautiful girls, the abandoned hours?
They said we were lost, mad and immoral,
And interfered with the plans of the management.
And today, millions and millions, shut alive
In the coffins of circumstance,
Beat on the buried lids,
Huddle in the cellars of ruins, and quarrel
Over their own fragmented flesh.

GAS OR NOVOCAIN

Here I sit, reading the Stoic
Latin of Tacitus.
Tiberius sinks in senile
Gloom as Aeneas sank
In the smoky throat of Hades;
And the prose glitters like
A tray of dental instruments.
The toss head president,
Deep in his private catacomb,
Is preparing to pull
The trigger. His secretaries
Make speeches. In ten years
The art of communication
Will be more limited.
The wheel, the lever, the incline,
May survive, and perhaps,
The alphabet. At the moment
The intellectual
Advance guard is agitated
Over the relation
Between the Accumulation
Of Capital and the
Systematic Derangement of
The Senses, and the Right
To Homosexuality.

IT ROLLS ON

Irresolute, pausing on a doubtful journey;
Once more, after so long, the unique autumnal
Wonder of the upper Hudson about me;
I walk in the long forgotten
Familiar garden. The house was never
Reoccupied, the windows are broken,
The walks and the arbors ruinous,
The flower beds are thickets,
The hedges are shattered,
The quince and hawthorns broken and dying.
One by one the memories of twenty years
Vanish and there is no trace of them.
I have been restless in many places
Since I rested in this place.
The dry thickets are full of migrating
Grey green warblers. Since last fall
They have visited Guatemala and Labrador
And now they are bound south again.
Their remote ancestors were doing the same thing
When I was here before. Each generation
Has stopped for an autumn evening
Here, in this place, each year.

DELIA REXROTH

Died June, 1916

Under your illkempt yellow roses,
Delia, today you are younger
Than your son. Two and a half decades—
The family monument sagged askew,
And he overtook your half-a-life.
On the other side of the country,
Near the willows by the slow river,
Deep in the earth, the white ribs retain
The curve of your fervent, careful breast;
The fine skull, the ardor of your brain.
And in the fingers the memory
Of Chopin études, and in the feet
Slow waltzes and champagne twosteps sleep.
And the white full moon of midsummer,
That you watched awake all that last night,
Watches history fill the deserts
And oceans with corpses once again;
And looks in the east window at me,
As I move past you to middle age
And knowledge past your agony and waste.

ANOTHER ONE

Septimius, the forms you know so well,
The olla of callas, the multiform
Guitar, the svelte girl torso and slick thigh,
Surprise you and become you unaware.
You get drunk like one of your spotless nudes;
I hear that you resemble a still life
Between sheets; and your conversation ticks
From certitude to tock;
But not with me.

ANDREE REXROTH

Died October, 1940

Now once more gray mottled buckeye branches
Explode their emerald stars,
And alders smoulder in a rosy smoke
Of innumerable buds.
I know that spring again is splendid
As ever, the hidden thrush
As sweetly tongued, the sun as vital—
But these are the forest trails we walked together,
These paths, ten years together.
We thought the years would last forever,
They are all gone now, the days
We thought would not come for us are here.
Bright trout poised in the current—
The raccoon's track at the water's edge—
A bittern booming in the distance—
Your ashes scattered on this mountain—
Moving seaward on this stream.

PRECESSION OF THE EQUINOXES

Time was, I walked in February rain,
My head full of its own rhythms like a shell,
And came home at night to write of love and death,
High philosophy, and brotherhood of man.

After intimate acquaintance with these things,
I contemplate the changes of the weather,
Flowers, birds, rabbits, mice and other small deer
Fulfilling the year's periodicity.

And the reassurances of my own pulse.

AGAIN AT WALDHEIM

"Light upon Waldheim"
Voltairine de Cleyre on the Haymarket martyrs

How heavy the heart is now, and every heart
Save only the word drunk, power drunk
Hard capsule of the doomed. How distraught
Those things of pride, the wills nourished in the fat
Years, fed in the kindly twilight of the books
In gold and brown, the voices that had little
To live for, crying for something to die for.
The philosophers of history,
Of dim wit and foolish memory,
The giggling concubines of catastrophe—
Who forget so much—Boethius' calm death,
More's sweet speech, Rosa's broken body—
Or you, tough, stubby recalcitrant
Of Fate.

      Now in Waldheim where the rain
Has fallen careless and unthinking
For all an evil century's youth,
Where now the banks of dark roses lie,
What memory lasts, Emma, of you,
Or of the intrepid comrades of your grave,
Of Piotr, of "mutual aid,"
Against the iron clad flame throwing
Course of time?
        Your stakes were on the turn
Of a card whose face you knew you would not see.

You knew that nothing could ever be
More desperate than truth; and when every voice
Was cowed, you spoke against the coalitions
For the duration of the emergency—
In the permanent emergency
You spoke for the irrefutable
Coalition of the blood of men.

STRENGTH THROUGH JOY

Coming back over the col between
Isosceles Mountain and North Palisade,
I stop at the summit and look back
At the storm gathering over the white peaks
Of the Whitney group and the colored
Kaweahs. September, nineteen-thirty-nine.
This is the last trip in the mountains
This autumn, possibly the last trip ever.
The storm clouds rise up the mountainside,
Lightning batters the pinnacles above me,
The clouds beneath the pass are purple
And I see rising through them from the valleys
And cities a cold, murderous flood,
Spreading over the world, lapping at the last
Inviolate heights; mud streaked yellow
With gas, slimy and blotched with crimson,
Filled with broken bits of steel and flesh,
Moving slowly with the blind motion
Of lice, spreading inexorably
As bacteria spread in tissues,
Swirling with the precise rapacity of starved rats.
I loiter here like a condemned man
Lingers over his last breakfast, his last smoke;
Thinking of those heroes of the war
Of human skill, foresight, endurance and will;
The disinterested bravery,
The ideal combat of peace: Bauer
Crawling all night around his icecave
On snowbound Kanchenjunga, Tilman
And Shipton skylarking on Nanda Devi,
Smythe seeing visions on Everest,
The mad children of the Eigerwand—
What holidays will they keep this year?
Gun emplacements blasted in the rock;
No place for graves, the dead covered with quicklime

Or left in the snow till the spring thaw;
Machine gun duels between white robed ski troops,
The last screaming schusses marked with blood.
Was it for this we spent the years perfecting
The craft of courage? Better the corpse
Of the foolhardy, frozen on the Eiger
Accessible only to the storm,
Standing sentry for the avalanche.

STILL ON WATER

Solitude closes down around us
As we lie passive and exhausted
Solitude clamps us softly in its warm hand.
A turtle slips into the water
With a faint noise like a breaking bubble;
There is no other sound, only the dim
Momentous conversation of windless
Poplar and sycamore leaves and rarely,
A single, questioning frog voice.
I turn my eyes from your entranced face
And watch the oncoming sunset
Powder the immense, unblemished zenith
With almost imperceptible sparkles of gold.
Your eyes open, your head turns.
Your lips nibble at my shoulder.
I feel a languid shudder run over your body.
Suddenly you laugh, like a pure
Exulting flute, spring to your feet
And plunge into the water.
A white bird breaks from the rushes
And flies away, and the boat rocks
Drunkenly in the billows
Of your nude jubilation.

UN BEL DI VEDREMO

"Hello NBC, this is London speaking . . ."
I move the dial, I have heard it all,
Day after day—the terrible waiting,
The air raids, the military communiqués,
The between the lines whispering
Of quarreling politicians,
The mute courage of the people.
The dial moves over aggressive
Advertisements, comedians, bands hot and sweet,
To a record concert—La Scala—Madame Butterfly.
I pause, listening idly, and suddenly
I feel as though I had begun to fall
Slowly, buoyantly, through infinite, indefinite space.
Milano, fretting in my seat,
In my lace collar and velvet suit,
My beautiful mother weeping
Happily beside me. My God,
How long ago it was, further far
Than Rome or Egypt, that other
World before the other war.
Stealing downstairs to spy on the champagne suppers;
Watching the blue flame of the chafing dish
On Sunday nights: driving over middle Europe
Behind a café au lait team,
The evenings misty, smelling of cattle
And the fat Danubian earth.
It will never be again
The open work stockings,
The lace evening gowns,
The pink roses on the slippers;
Debs eating roast chicken and drinking whiskey,
On the front porch with grandpa;
The neighbors gaping behind their curtains;
The Japanese prints and the works of Huneker.
Never again will a small boy
Curled in the hammock in the murmurous summer air,

Gnaw his knuckles, reading *The Jungle*;
Never again will he gasp as Franz Josef
And the princesses sweep through
The lines of wolf caped hussars.
It is a terrible thing to sit here
In the uneasy light above this strange city
And listen to the poignant sentimentality
Of an age more dead than the Cro Magnon.
It is a terrible thing to see a world die twice,
"The first time as tragedy,
The second as evil farce."

ADONIS IN WINTER

Persephone awaits him in the dim boudoir,
Waits him, for the hour is at hand.
She has arranged the things he likes
Near to his expected hand:
Herrick's poems, tobacco, the juice
Of pomegranates in a twisted glass.
She piles her drugged blonde hair
Above her candid forehead,
Touches up lips and eyelashes,
Selects her most naked robe.
On the stroke of the equinox he comes,
And smiles, and stretches his arms, and strokes
Her cheeks and childish shoulders, and kisses
The violet lids closed on the grey eyes.
Free of aggressive Aphrodite,
Free of the patronizing gods,
The cruel climate of Olympus,
They feed caramels to Cerberus
And warn him not to tell
The cuckold Pluto of their adulteries,
Their mortal lechery in dispassionate Hell.

ADONIS IN SUMMER

The Lotophagi with their silly hands
Haunt me in sleep, plucking at my sleeve;
Their gibbering laughter and blank eyes
Hide on the edge of the mind's vision
In dusty subways and crowded streets.
Late in August, asleep, Adonis
Appeared to me, frenzied and bleeding
And showed me, clutched in his hand, the plow
That broke the dream of Persephone.
The next day, regarding the scorched grass
In the wilting park, I became aware
That beneath me, beneath the gravel
And the hurrying ants, and the loam
And the subsoil, lay the glacial drift,
The Miocene jungles, the reptiles
Of the Jurassic, the cuttlefish
Of the Devonian, Cambrian
Worms, and the mysteries of the gneiss;
Their histories folded, docketed
In darkness; and deeper still the hot
Black core of iron, and once again
The inscrutable archaic rocks,
And the long geologic ladder,
And the living soil and the strange trees,
And the tangled bodies of lovers
Under the strange stars.
   And beside me,
A mad old man, plucking at my sleeve.

WEDNESDAY OF HOLY WEEK, 1940

Out of the east window a storm
Blooms spasmodically across the moonrise;
In the west, in the haze, the planets
Pulsate like standing meteors.
We listen in the darkness to the service of Tenebrae,
Music older than the Resurrection,
The voice of the ruinous, disorderly Levant:
"Why doth the city sit solitary
That was full of people?"
The voices of the Benedictines are massive, impersonal;
They neither fear this agony nor are ashamed of it.
Think . . . six hours ago in Europe,
Thousands were singing these words,
Putting out the candles psalm by psalm . . .
Albi like a fort in the cold dark,
Aachen, the voices fluttering in the ancient vaulting,
The light of the last candle
In Munich on the gnarled carving.
"Jerusalem, Jerusalem,
Return ye unto the Lord thy God."
Thousands kneeling in the dark,
Saying, "Have mercy upon me O God."
We listen appreciatively, smoking, talking quietly,
The voices are coming from three thousand miles.
On the white garden wall the shadows
Of the date palm thresh wildly;
The full moon of the spring is up,
And a gale with it.

INCARNATION

Climbing alone all day long
In the blazing waste of spring snow,
I came down with the sunset's edge
To the highest meadow, green
In the cold mist of waterfalls,
To a cobweb of water
Woven with innumerable
Bright flowers of wild iris;
And saw far down our fire's smoke
Rising between the canyon walls,
A human thing in the empty mountains.
And as I stood on the stones
In the midst of whirling water,
The whirling iris perfume
Caught me in a vision of you
More real than reality:
Fire in the deep curves of your hair:
Your hips whirled in a tango,
Out and back in dim scented light;
Your cheeks snow-flushed, the zithers
Ringing, all the crowded ski lodge
Dancing and singing; your arms
White in the brown autumn water,
Swimming through the fallen leaves,
Making a fluctuant cobweb
Of light on the sycamores;
Your thigh's exact curve, the fine gauze
Slipping through my hands, and you
Tense on the verge of abandon;
Your breasts' very touch and smell;
The sweet secret odor of sex.
Forever the thought of you,
And the splendor of the iris,
The crinkled iris petal,
The gold hairs powdered with pollen,
And the obscure cantata

Of the tangled water, and the
Burning, impassive snow peaks,
Are knotted together here.
This moment of fact and vision
Seizes immortality,
Becomes the person of this place.
The responsibility
Of love realized and beauty
Seen burns in a burning angel
Real beyond flower or stone.

WE COME BACK

Now, on this day of the first hundred flowers,
Fate pauses for us in imagination,
As it shall not ever in reality—
As these swifts that link endless parabolas
Change guard unseen in their secret crevices.
Other anniversaries that we have walked
Along this hillcrest through the black fir forest,
Past the abandoned farm, have been just the same—
Even the fog necklaces on the fencewires
Seem to have gained or lost hardly a jewel;
The annual and diurnal patterns hold.
Even the attrition of the cypress grove
Is slow and orderly, each year one more tree
Breaks ranks and lies down, decrepit in the wind.
Each year, on summer's first luminous morning,
The swallows come back, whispering and weaving
Figure eights around the sharp curves of the swifts,
Plaiting together the summer air all day,
That the bats and owls unravel in the nights.
And we come back, the signs of time upon us,
In the pause of fate, the threading of the year.

MARTIAL — XII, LII

This is your own lover, Kenneth, Marie,
Who someday will be part of the earth
Beneath your feet; who crowned you once with roses
Of song; whose voice was no less famous
Raised against the guilt of his generation.
Sweetly in Hell he'll tell your story
To the enraptured ears of Helen,
Our joys and jealousies, our quarrels and journeys,
That unlike hers, ended in kisses.
Her spouse will smile at impetuous Paris
When he hears the tale of our sweet lust.
Laura and Petrarca, Waller and his Rose,
Grim Dante and glowing Beatrice,
Catullus and Lesbia, and all the rest,
Transparent hand in hand, will listen,
A tremor on their shadowy flesh once more.
And when at last I welcome you there
Your name will stand for memory of living
On the tongues of all whom death has joined.
You shall know this when you see my grave snowless
Winter long, and my cold sleepfellows
Shifting themselves underground to warm
Dead bones at my still glowing ashes.

THEORY OF NUMBERS

Think, as we lie in this sweet bed,
With the lamplight dim on books
And pictures of three thousand years,
And the light caught in the wine
Like Mars or Aldebaran:
Vaulted over the winter mountains,
The night sky is like the pure
Space of the imagination—

Defined by infinite star points,
Interrupted by meteors,
And the fleshy fires of planets
That move like infusoria.
The moon is as sheer as glass;
Its globe dissolves in illusion;
Out from it flow mysterious
Lines and surfaces, folding
And unfolding without limit.
The *Carmina Burana*—
Differential geometry—
"Dum Dianae vitrea
While Diana's crystal lamp"
Proof of the questionable
Existence of integrals—
And this bloody sacrament,
This linking of corpuscles
Like atoms of oxygen,
This Matrimony called Holy,
This is the lens of intention,
Focusing liability
From world to person, from passion
To action; and conversely,
The source of potential in fact.
The individual—the world—
On the bookshelves there is only
Paper soiled by history.
The space of night is infinite,
The blackness and emptiness
Crossed only by thin bright fences
Of logic.
                    Lying under
The night sky's inexhaustible
Equation, and fallen from it,
Uncountable hexagons
Of snow blanket the streamlined
Volcanic stones, and the columns
Of hexagonal basalt,
And the hexagons of wax
And honey where the bees sleep.

ANDREE REXROTH

Purple and green, blue and white,
The Oregon river mouths
Slide into thick smoky darkness
As the turning cup of day
Slips from the whirling hemisphere.
And all that white long beach gleams
In white twilight as the lights
Come on in the lonely hamlets;
And voices of men emerge;
And dogs barking, as the wind stills.
Those August evenings are
Sixteen years old tonight and I
Am sixteen years older too—
Lonely, caught in the midst of life,
In the chaos of the world;
And all the years that we were young
Are gone, and every atom
Of your learned and disordered
Flesh is utterly consumed.

HORNY DILEMMA

I have long desired to shine
As the modern Juvenal.
However, when I survey
The vast jungle infested
With bushmasters and tsetse
Flies imperviously stretched
From A . . . B . . . to C . . . .
D . . . . E . . . , from M . . . .
N . . . . , to Y . . . . Z . . . . . ,
I resign myself perforce
To Martial's brief excursions.

INCENSE

Her boudoir is ornamented with
The works of the Bloomsbury mystics—
Limited editions in warped vellum;
There is also a mauve draped prie-dieu
And a New Mexican crucifix.
Sinister and intimidating
As this environment might appear,
Her ecstasies can be distinguished
From those of Lais the agnostic
Only by their singular frequency.

A NEOCLASSICIST

I know your moral sources, prig.
Last night you plunged awake screaming.
You dreamed you'd grown extremely old,
Lay dying, and to your deathbed,
All the girls you'd ever slept with
Came, as old as you, to watch you die.
Comatose, your blotched residues
Shrivelled and froze between stiff sheets;
And the faces, dim as under
Dirty water, incurious,
Silent, of a room full of old,
Old women, waited, patiently.

PAST AND FUTURE
TURN ABOUT

Autumn has returned and we return
To the same beach in the last hours.
The Phoenix and the Tortoise is finished.
The gratuitous discipline of finality
Falls on our lives and shapes our ends.
Ourselves as objectives, our objects,
Pass from our hands to the hands of time.
Reconsidering and revising
My life and the meaning of my poem,
I gather once more within me
The old material, sea and stone.

The green spring that comes in November.
With the first rains has restored the hills.
Seals are playing in the kelp beds.
As the surf sweeps in they can be seen
Weaving over one another in
The standing water. In the granite
Cliffs are swarms of dark fish shaped patches
Of rock oriented to the flow lines
Of the hot magma. Nobody knows
Exactly what caused their formation,
Deep in the blind earth under the blind
Jurassic world, under the dead
Franciscan series, what disorder,
What process. On the wet sand lie
Hundreds of jellyfish with pale
Lavender organs at their hearts.
The sun will dry them and leave only
A brittle film. There are more hundreds
Pulsing through the water, struggling
Against the drive of the rising tide.
Down the beach beyond a tangle
Of barbed wire an armed sentry stands,
Gazing seaward under his helmet.

Carapace or transfiguration—
History will doubtless permit us
Neither. Eventually the will
Exhausts itself and turns, seeking grace,
To the love that suffers ignorance
And time's irresponsibility.
The Cross cannot be climbed upon.
It cannot be seized like a weapon
Against the injustice of the world.
"No one has ever seized injustice
In his bare hands and bent it back.
No one has ever tried to smash evil,
Without smashing himself and sinking
Into greater evil or despair."
The Satanic cunning represents
Itself as very strong, but just
A trifle weaker than its victim.
This is the meaning of temptation.
The Devil does not fool with fools.

It is easy to read or write
In a book, "Self realization
Is responsible self sacrifice."
"The will to power, the will to live,
Are fulfilled by transfiguration."
"The person is the final value;
Value is responsibility."
As the world sinks in a marsh of blood,
You won't raise yourself by your bootstraps,
However pious and profound.
Christ was not born of Socrates,
But to a disorderly people,
In an evil time, in the flesh
Of innocence and humility.

"The self determining will." What self?
What determination? History
Plays its pieces—"The Japanese
Adventure was shaped on the countless
G'oto tables of a hundred years."

Black slowly immobilizes white.
Evil reveals its hidden aces.
As the Philosopher observes,
"Fear is the sentiment of men
Beaten and overcome in mind,
Confronted by an imminent evil
Which they take to be too much for them
To resist and more than they can bear."
And again, appropriately, in the Rhetoric,
"We are never afraid of evil
When we are in the thick of it
And all chance of escape has vanished.
Fear always looks to flight, and catches
With the fancy's eye some glimpse
Of an opening for the avoidance
Of evil."

        "O my Father, all things
Are possible unto Thee, if it be
Possible let this cup pass from me.
Nevertheless, not my will, but Thine."

The self determining will accepts
The responsibility of all
Contingency. What will? What self?
The Cross descends into the world
Like a sword, but the hilt thereof
Is in the heavens. Every man
Is his own Adam, left to itself,
The self unselfs itself, the will
Demands autonomy and achieves
It by a system of strategic
Retreats—the inane autonomy
Of the morally neuter event.
Conversion, penitence, and grace—
Autonomy is a by product
Of identification.

What was our sacrifice worth?
Practically nothing, the waste
Of time overwhelms heroes,
Pyramids and catastrophes.
Who knows the tropical foci
Of the Jurassic ice flows?
Who has seen the frozen black mass
That rushes upon us biding
Its light years? Who remembers
The squad that died stopping the tanks
At the bridgehead? The company
Was bombed out an hour later.
Simonides is soon forgotten.
The pressure of the unfound
Future is the pressure of the lost
Past, the brain stiffens with hope,
And swims in hallucination
Beating its spinal column
Like a flagellate in a mild
Solution of alcohol,
And pressed against it, mantis
To mantis, the cobwebbed body—
The caput abdominale.
As for that thin entelechy,
The person, let him wear the head
Of the wolf, in Sherwood Forest.

We return? Each to each, one
To another, each to the other?
Sweet lovely hallucination—
The sea falls through you, through the gulf
Of wish—last spring—what was value?
The hole itself cuts in its self
And watches as it fills with blood?
The waves of the sea fall through
Our each others indomitable
As peristalsis.

Autumn comes
And the death of flowers, but
The flowered colored waves of
The sea will last forever
Like the pattern on the dress
Of a beautiful woman.

Nineteen forty two and we
Are selves, stained, fixed and mounted
On the calendar—and the leaves
Fall easily in the gardens
Of a million ruins.

And deep
In the mountains the wind has stopped
The current of a stream with only
A windrow of the terribly
Red dogwood leaves.

THE SIGNATURE OF ALL THINGS

(1949)

For Marie

I cook young hearts
With overheated learning.
Eros is the starter of wisdom.
He lights the torches
Of the relay race of youth.

CEPHALOS

BETWEEN MYSELF AND DEATH

To Jimmy Blanton's Music:
Sophisticated Lady, Body and Soul

A fervor parches you sometimes,
And you hunch over it, silent,
Cruel, and timid; and sometimes
You are frightened with wantonness,
And give me your desperation.
Mostly we lurk in our coverts,
Protecting our spleens, pretending
That our bandages are our wounds.
But sometimes the wheel of change stops;
Illusion vanishes in peace;
And suddenly pride lights your flesh—
Lucid as diamond, wise as pearl—
And your face, remote, absolute,
Perfect and final like a beast's.
It is wonderful to watch you,
A living woman in a room
Full of frantic, sterile people,
And think of your arching buttocks
Under your velvet evening dress,
And the beautiful fire spreading
From your sex, burning flesh and bone,
The unbelievably complex
Tissues of your brain all alive
Under your coiling, splendid hair.

I like to think of you naked.
I put your naked body
Between myself alone and death.
If I go into my brain
And set fire to your sweet nipples,
To the tendons beneath your knees,
I can see far before me.

It is empty there where I look,
But at least it is lighted.

I know how your shoulders glisten,
How your face sinks into trance,
And your eyes like a sleepwalker's,
And your lips of a woman
Cruel to herself.
                    I like to
Think of you clothed, your body
Shut to the world and self contained,
Its wonderful arrogance
That makes all women envy you.
I can remember every dress,
Each more proud then a naked nun.
When I go to sleep my eyes
Close in a mesh of memory.
Its cloud of intimate odor
Dreams instead of myself.

MONADS

As the sun comes in the window,
And shines through the aquarium,
The water turns green in the light.
The swirling dinoflagellates
Make rockets in their own thick clouds,
Like the rockets that plunge along
The Yosemite waterfalls.
Lucretius, Leibniz—I wonder—
Are there windows in the flagellates?
I muse over an inward picture
Of the meteoric dust
Floating in the black sea deeps
And eddying in the sunlight
In the stratosphere.

THE SIGNATURE OF ALL THINGS

My head and shoulders, and my book
In the cool shade, and my body
Stretched bathing in the sun, I lie
Reading beside the waterfall—
Boehme's "Signature of all Things."
Through the deep July day the leaves
Of the laurel, all the colors
Of gold, spin down through the moving
Deep laurel shade all day. They float
On the mirrored sky and forest
For a while, and then, still slowly
Spinning, sink through the crystal deep
Of the pool to its leaf gold floor.
The saint saw the world as streaming
In the electrolysis of love.
I put him by and gaze through shade
Folded into shade of slender
Laurel trunks and leaves filled with sun.
The wren broods in her moss domed nest.
A newt struggles with a white moth
Drowning in the pool. The hawks scream,
Playing together on the ceiling
Of heaven. The long hours go by.
I think of those who have loved me,
Of all the mountains I have climbed,
Of all the seas I have swum in.
The evil of the world sinks.
My own sin and trouble fall away
Like Christian's bundle, and I watch
My forty summers fall like falling
Leaves and falling water held
Eternally in summer air.

Deer are stamping in the glades,
Under the full July moon.
There is a smell of dry grass
In the air, and more faintly,
The scent of a far off skunk.
As I stand at the wood's edge,
Watching the darkness, listening
To the stillness, a small owl
Comes to the branch above me,
On wings more still than my breath.
When I turn my light on him,
His eyes glow like drops of iron,
And he perks his head at me,
Like a curious kitten.
The meadow is bright as snow.
My dog prowls the grass, a dark
Blur in the blur of brightness.
I walk to the oak grove where
The Indian village was once.
There, in blotched and cobwebbed light
And dark, dim in the blue haze,
Are twenty Holstein heifers,
Black and white, all lying down,
Quietly together, under
The huge trees rooted in the graves.

When I dragged the rotten log
From the bottom of the pool,
It seemed heavy as stone.
I let it lie in the sun
For a month; and then chopped it
Into sections, and split them
For kindling, and spread them out
To dry some more. Late that night,
After reading for hours,
While moths rattled at the lamp—

The saints and the philosophers
On the destiny of man—
I went out on my cabin porch,
And looked up through the black forest
At the swaying islands of stars.
Suddenly I saw at my feet,
Spread on the floor of night, ingots
Of quivering phosphorescence,
And all about were scattered chips
Of pale cold light that was alive.

FOR A MASSEUSE AND PROSTITUTE

Nobody knows what love is anymore.
Nobody knows what happened to God.
After midnight, the lesbians and fairies
Sweep through the streets of the old tenderloin,
Like spirochetes in a softening brain.
The hustlers have all been run out of town.
I look back on the times spent
Talking with you about the idiocies
Of a collapsing world and the brutalities
Of my race and yours,
While the sick, the perverted, the malformed,
Came and went, and you cooked them,
And rolled them, and beat them,
And sent them away with a little taste
Of electric life from the ends of your fingers.
Who could ever forget your amiable body,
Or your unruffled good sense,
Or your smiling sex?
I suppose your touch kept many men
As sane as they could be kept.
Every hour there is less of that touch in the world.

LYELL'S HYPOTHESIS AGAIN

An Attempt to Explain the Former Changes of the Earth's Surface by Causes Now in Operation
Subtitle of Lyell: Principles of Geology

The mountain road ends here,
Broken away in the chasm where
The bridge washed out years ago.
The first scarlet larkspur glitters
In the first patch of April
Morning sunlight. The engorged creek
Roars and rustles like a military
Ball. Here by the waterfall,
Insuperable life, flushed
With the equinox, sentient
And sentimental, falls away
To the sea and death. The tissue
Of sympathy and agony
That binds the flesh in its Nessus' shirt;
The clotted cobweb of unself
And self; sheds itself and flecks
The sun's bed with darts of blossom
Like flagellant blood above
The water bursting in the vibrant
Air. This ego, bound by personal
Tragedy and the vast
Impersonal vindictiveness
Of the ruined and ruining world,
Pauses in this immortality,
As passionate, as apathetic,
As the lava flow that burned here once;
And stopped here; and said, 'This far
And no further.' And spoke thereafter
In the simple diction of stone.

Naked in the warm April air,
We lie under the redwoods,
In the sunny lee of a cliff.
As you kneel above me I see
Tiny red marks on your flanks
Like bites, where the redwood cones
Have pressed into your flesh.
You can find just the same marks
In the lignite in the cliff
Over our heads. *Sequoia
Langsdorfii* before the ice,
And *sempervirens* afterwards,
There is little difference,
Except for all those years.

Here in the sweet, moribund
Fetor of spring flowers, washed,
Flotsam and jetsam together,
Cool and naked together,
Under this tree for a moment,
We have escaped the bitterness
Of love, and love lost, and love
Betrayed. And what might have been,
And what might be, fall equally
Away with what is, and leave
Only these ideograms
Printed on the immortal
Hydrocarbons of flesh and stone.

SHARP IN MY HEART

Come, O my love, and lay you down.
Come, O my love, and lay you down.
The summer is gone,
And the leaves turn brown.

The summer is gone, and the leaves fall down.
The summer is gone, and the leaves fall down.
I loved you well,
And you did me wrong.

I loved you well, and you broke my heart.
I loved you well, and you broke my heart.
Love me once more,
And forever part.

Love me once more, though I know you lie.
Love me once more, though I know you lie.
Leave me a memory
For the day I die.

Leave me a memory that I can't forget.
Leave me a memory that I can't forget.
I can see those hours
Go past us yet.

I can see those hours, as the summer drew near.
I can see those hours, as the summer drew near.
Sharp in my heart,
Like diamonds clear.

Sharp in my heart, the leaves turn green.
Sharp in my heart, the leaves turn green.
Your innocent face
I wish I never had seen.

Tune: in Matteson and Henry, *Beech Mountain*
Folk-Songs and Ballads, Schirmer, N. Y., 1936.

BLUES

The tops of the higher peaks
Of the Sierra Nevada
Of California are
Drenched in the perfume of
A flower which grows only there —
The blue *Polemonium
Confertum eximium,*
Soft, profound blue, like the eyes
Of impregnable innocence;
The perfume is heavy and
Clings thickly to the granite
Peaks, even in violent wind;
The leaves are clustered,
Fine, dull green, sticky, and musky.
I imagine that the scent
Of the body of Artemis
That put Endymion to sleep
Was like this and her eyes had the
Same inscrutable color.
Lawrence was lit into death
By the blue gentians of Kore.
Vanzetti had in his cell
A bowl of tall blue flowers
From a New England garden.
I hope that when I need it
My mind can always call back
This flower to its hidden senses.

YUGAO

Tonight is clearer and colder.
The new half moon slides through clouds.
The air is full of the poignant
Odor of frost drying earth.
Late night, the stillness grows more still.
At last, nothing moves, no sound,
Even the shunting freight trains
In the distance stop.
                                    I go out
Into the ominous dark,
Into the garden crowded with
Invisible, impalpable
Movement. The air is breathless
Under the trees. High overhead,
The wind plunges with the moon
Through breaking and driving clouds.
I seem to stand in the midst
Of an incomprehensible
Tragedy; as though a world
Doubled against this were tearing
Through the thin shell of night;
As though something earth bound with its
Own glamorous violence
Struggled beside me in the dark.
On such nights as this the young
Warriors of old time take form
In the Noh plays; and, it may be,
Some distraught, imagined girl,
Amalfi's duchess, Electra,
Struggles like an ice bound swan,
Out of the imagination,
Toward a body, beside me,
Beyond the corner of the eye;
Or, may be, some old jealousy
Or hate I have forgotten
Still seeks flesh to walk in life.

If so, I cannot see her.
I can call, plain to the mind's eye,
Your bright sleeping head, nested
In its pillow, and your face, sure
And peaceful as your moving
Breath. You, wandering in your dream,
Watched over by your love for me.

JANUARY NIGHT

LATE, AFTER WALKING FOR HOURS ON THE BEACH, A STORM RISES, WITH WIND, RAIN AND LIGHTNING

In front of me on my desk
Is typewriter and paper,
And my beautiful jagged
Crystal, larger than a skull,
And beyond, the black window,
Framing the wet and swarming
Pointillism of the city
In the night, in the valley
And spread on the distant hills
Under the rain, and beyond,
Thin rivulets of lightning
Trickling down the sky,
And all the intervening
Air wet with the fecundity
Of time and the promises
Of the earth and its routine
Annual and diurnal
Yearly and daily changeless
Motion; and once more my hours
Turn in the trough of winter
And climb towards the sun.

DELIA REXROTH

California rolls into
Sleepy summer, and the air
Is full of the bitter sweet
Smoke of the grass fires burning
On the San Francisco hills.
Flesh burns so, and the pyramids
Likewise, and the burning stars.
Tired tonight, in a city
Of parvenus, in the inhuman
West, in the most blood drenched year,
I took down a book of poems
That you used to like, that you
Used to sing to music I
Never found anywhere again —
Michael Field's book, *Long Ago*.
Indeed it's long ago now —
Your bronze hair and svelte body.
I guess you were a fierce lover,
A wild wife, an animal
Mother. And now life has cost
Me more years, though much less pain,
Than you had to pay for it.
And I have bought back, for and from
Myself, these poems and paintings,
Carved from the protesting bone,
The precious consequences
Of your torn and distraught life.

HOJOKI

Venus in the pale green sky
Where the Pleiades glimmer
Under a bar of dark cloud,
The moon travels through the L
Formed by Jupiter and Saturn
In conjunction below Gemini —
The year marches through the stars
Orion again walks into the sea.
The horned owl sits on the tree
By my hut and watches me
As I gather a handful
Of sticks and boil my rice.
He stays there through the growing dusk,
I can hardly see him when
He flies off in the starlight.

SPRING

Fine warm rain falls through the maple
And laurel leaves, and fills the narrow
Gorge with a pulse like life.
The waterfall is muffled,
And my ten foot square hut lies
In the abysm of a sea
Of sibilant quiet.

AUTUMN

I lay aside the Diurnal
At the light drenched poetry
Of St. Ambrose that converted
St. Augustine to a world
More luminous and more lucid
Than one where light warred with dark.
I ponder what it is I find

Here by my hut in the speech
Of falling water's swift conjunction.
What have men ever found?
I think of Buddha's infinite
Laugh in the Lankavatara,
Lighting up all the universes.
The steep sides of the gorge enclose
Me like the thighs of a girl's
Body of bliss, and illusion,
And law. The end of dry autumn —
The narrow water whispers
Like the rustle of sheer, stiff silk.

SUMMER

A thing unknown for years,
Rain falls heavily in June,
On the ripe cherries, and on
The half cut hay.
Above the glittering
Grey water of the inlet,
In the driving, light filled mist,
A blue heron
Catches mice in the green
And copper and citron swathes.
I walk on the rainy hills.
It is enough.

WINTER

Very late, a thin wash
Of cirrus cloud covers half
The sky and obscures
A three quarter moon.
Since midnight it has turned warmer.
There will be rain before morning.
There is no wind.
Everything holds still
In the vaporous light.

I walk along the stream.
Its voices are rich and subdued.
The alders overhead blend their bare twigs
And catkins with the moonlit clouds
Into one indistinct, netted haze.
The hills, covered with wet young grass,
Are intangible as billows of fog.
The decaying leaves on the path
Break the light into a hazy shimmer.
The thin bladed laurel leaves
Look like Su Tung Po's bamboos.
Two deer bounce away from me
Through the woods, in and out
Of the shadows like puffs of smoke.
The moon grows very dim.
The air does not move at all.
The stream deepens its voices.
I turn to go back to my hut,
And come on the cloudy moon
And the light filled sky
Reflected through the bare branches
In a boundless, velvety pool.
I stand and gaze and remember
That if this were my home country,
In a few hours, slow, still, wet, huge,
Flakes of snow would be falling
Through the windless dawn.

SPRING

I sit under the old oak,
And gaze at the white orchard,
In bloom under the full moon.
The oak purrs like a lion,
And seems to quiver and breathe.
I am startled until I
Realize that the beehive
In the hollow trunk will be
Busy all night long tonight.

ANDREE REXROTH

The years have gone. It is spring
Again. Mars and Saturn will
Soon come on, low in the West,
In the dusk. Now the evening
Sunlight makes hazy girders
Over Steep Ravine above
The waterfalls. The winter
Birds from Oregon, robins
And varied thrushes, feast on
Ripe toyon and madroñe
Berries. The robins sing as
The dense light falls.

                Your ashes
Were scattered in this place. Here
I wrote you a farewell poem,
And long ago another,
A poem of peace and love,
Of the lassitude of a long
Spring evening in youth. Now
It is almost ten years since
You came here to stay. Once more,
The pussy willows that come
After the New Year in this
Outlandish land are blooming.
There are deer and raccoon tracks
In the same places. A few
New sand bars and cobble beds
Have been left where erosion
Has gnawed deep into the hills.
The rounds of life are narrow.
War and peace have past like ghosts.
The human race sinks towards
Oblivion. A bittern

Calls from the same rushes where
You heard one on our first year
In the West; and where I heard
One again in the year
Of your death.

KINGS RIVER CANYON

My sorrow is so wide
I cannot see across it;
And so deep I shall never
Reach the bottom of it.
The moon sinks through deep haze,
As though the Kings River Canyon
Were filled with fine, warm, damp gauze.
Saturn gleams through the thick light
Like a gold, wet eye; nearby,
Antares glows faintly,
Without sparkle. Far overhead,
Stone shines darkly in the moonlight —
Lookout Point, where we lay
In another full moon, and first
Peered down into this canyon.
Here we camped, by still autumnal
Pools, all one warm October.
I baked you a bannock birthday cake.
Here you did your best paintings —
Innocent, wondering landscapes.
Very few of them are left
Anywhere. You destroyed them
In the terrible trouble
Of your long sickness. Eighteen years
Have passed since that autumn.
There was no trail here then.
Only a few people knew
How to enter this canyon.
We were all alone, twenty
Miles from anybody;

A young husband and wife,
Closed in and wrapped about
In the quiet autumn,
In the sound of quiet water,
In the turning and falling leaves,
In the wavering of innumerable
Bats from the caves, dipping
Over the odorous pools
Where the great trout drowsed in the evenings.

Eighteen years have been ground
To pieces in the wheels of life.
You are dead. With a thousand
Convicts they have blown a highway
Through Horseshoe Bend. Youth is gone,
That only came once. My hair
Is turning grey and my body
Heavier. I too move on to death.
I think of Henry King's stilted
But desolated *Exequy*,
Of Yuan Chen's great poem,
Unbearably pitiful;
Alone by the Spring river
More alone than I had ever
Imagined I would ever be,
I think of Frieda Lawrence,
Sitting alone in New Mexico,
In the long drought, listening
For the hiss of the milky Isar,
Over the cobbles, in a lost Spring.

A LETTER TO
WILLIAM CARLOS WILLIAMS

Dear Bill,

When I search the past for you,
Sometimes I think you are like
St. Francis, whose flesh went out
Like a happy cloud from him,
And merged with every lover —
Donkeys, flowers, lepers, suns —
But I think you are more like
Brother Juniper, who suffered
All indignities and glories
Laughing like a gentle fool.
You're in the *Fioretti*
Somewhere, for you're a fool, Bill,
Like the Fool in Yeats, the term
Of all wisdom and beauty.
It's you, stands over against
Helen in all her wisdom,
Solomon in all his glory.

Remember years ago, when
I told you you were the first
Great Franciscan poet since
The Middle Ages? I disturbed
The even tenor of dinner.
Your wife thought I was crazy.
It's true, though. And you're 'pure', too,
A real classic, though not loud
About it—a whole lot like
The girls of the Anthology.
Not like strident Sappho, who
For all her grandeur, must have
Had endemetriosis,
But like Anyte, who says
Just enough, softly, for all
The thousands of years to remember.

It's a wonderful quiet
You have, a way of keeping
Still about the world, and its
Dirty rivers, and garbage cans,
Red wheelbarrows glazed with rain,
Cold plums stolen from the icebox,
And Queen Anne's lace, and day's eyes,
And leaf buds bursting over
Muddy roads, and splotched bellies
With babies in them, and Cortes
And Malinche on the bloody
Causeway, the death of the flower world.

Nowadays, when the press reels
With chatterboxes, you keep still,
Each year a sheaf of stillness,
Poems that have nothing to say,
Like the stillness of George Fox,
Sitting still under the cloud
Of all the world's temptation,
By the fire, in the kitchen,
In the Vale of Beavor. And
The archetype, the silence
Of Christ, when he paused a long
Time and then said, 'Thou sayest it'.

Now in a recent poem you say,
'I who am about to die.'
Maybe this is just a tag
From the classics, but it sends
A shudder over me. Where
Do you get that stuff, Williams?
Look at here. The day will come
When a young woman will walk
By the lucid Williams River,
Where it flows through an idyllic
News from Nowhere sort of landscape,
And she will say to her children,
'Isn't it beautiful? It

Is named after a man who
Walked here once when it was called
The Passaic, and was filthy
With the poisonous excrements
Of sick men and factories.
He was a great man. He knew
It was beautiful then, although
Nobody else did, back there
In the Dark Ages. And the
Beautiful river he saw
Still flows in his veins, as it
Does in ours, and flows in our eyes,
And flows in time, and makes us
Part of it, and part of him.
That, children, is what is called
A sacramental relationship.
And that is what a poet
Is, children, one who creates
Sacramental relationships
That last always.'
  With love and admiration,
  Kenneth Rexroth.

MAXIMIAN, ELEGY V

for Mildred

The sky is perfectly clear.
Motionless in the moonlight,
The redwood forest descends
Three thousand feet to the sea,
To the unmoving, silent,
Thick, white fog bank that stretches
Westward to the horizon.
No sound rises from the sea;
And the forest is soundless.
Here in the open windows,

Watching the night together,
I cannot understand what
You murmur, singing sweetly,
Softly, to yourself, in French.
O, lady, you are learned,
In your hands as they touch me,
In lips that sing obscurely,
In secret, your private songs.
Your face looks white and frozen
In the moonlight, and your eyes
Glitter, rigid and immense.
The illusion of moonlight
Makes you look terror stricken.
And behind you the firelight
Draws black and red frightening
Toppling patterns on the walls.
An airplane crosses, low down,
And fills the landscape with noise
Like an hallucination.
Alive or dead, the stiff heart,
As the hours slide through moonlight,
Squeezes blood and memory.
The fog climbs up the mountain,
And leaves only one star in
The fog bound wood, like an eye
In a tomb. Without warning
Your voice breaks, and your face
Streams with tears, and you stagger
Against me. I do not speak,
But hold you still in my arms.
Finally you say, 'I am not
Weeping for our own troubles,
But for the general chaos
Of the world.' I feel you hurling
Away, abandoned on
A parachute of ruin.
A violent shuddering
Overcomes me, as though all
The women like you who had
Ever lived, had stepped across my grave.

BLOOD AND SAND

If there ever was a spoiled darling,
It was you, García-Lorca.
The sensation of three continents,
That was you, García-Lorca.
You were asked to dinner everywhere.
You were divine, Federico.
What went on in you, Federico,
Orestes doubling for Dwight Fiske?
Everyone threw his love at your head,
Those ailing loves, Federico,
With the channering worm in their garlands.
Hot Spain showed you her bare belly.
You saw the black solar plexus
Hollow with maggots. No love there.
No love. You made a concert program
Out of synonyms for agony,
The frightful parching agony
Of the lovers of Lot's wife.
You bore your own caesarian
Children daily, and all black stones.
They kept you pregnant, Federico,
With the chemicals of their unlust,
With their ugly devouring sperm,
With their pustulant, corrosive blood.
You watched the monster, Federico,
That Yeats saw stirring in the desert.
You never took your eyes off it.
It watched you, García-Lorca.
Then one day it walked. It never
Noticed you again, Federico.

THE GIANT WEAPON

YVOR WINTERS' NEW BOOK COMES ON THE
ANNIVERSARY OF THE DAY THAT I MET MY
WIFE. WE READ IT WHILE TROOP TRAINS MOVE
IN THE VALLEY BELOW US.

Today *The Giant Weapon* came,
Fresh from the press, and fresh
From fifteen years' growth and decay —
The annual sweet flesh
Of plums in the stunning summer,
Tightening each powdered line;
The sterile heat of autumn;
Lashing rain, and sharp wine,
And talk above disordered books
In winter evenings;
And the long wet forgetful walks
Under the swallows' wings,
Trillium past the orchard's edge;
Dogs drifting to old age;
Youth sifting over the children;
Time yellowing the page.
The Giant Weapon? The pattern?
The mind? The obdurate
Flesh? Or is it perhaps Janet
And you consecrate
In duality Plato said
Was the creative source
Of the many? Weapon or tool —
The wielded sovran force
Waste nor ruin shall overcome.
Flesh dead in lethal rain,
And the vain mind dissolved in hate,
Kisses at the dark train,
And children born of dead fathers,
And pressed flowers and blood
Stained snapshots—the creative will

Stirs the seed from the mud.
And the lost world we hunted, each
In proud flesh or tough mind,
Found, in doubled vision no cost
Of time or death shall blind.

FOR THE CHINESE ACTRESS,
GARDENIA CHANG

When Tu Fu was a small boy
He saw Kung Sung as she danced
With two swords, and years later
He remembered, and she lived
In his memory, always
Refining his perception,
As meditation on her
Sure grace had once taught Chang Hsu
The secret of powerful
And subtle calligraphy.
Now, days later, you are still
Clear and intact in my mind,
Your arch, small, transcendent face,
Your voice, so pure, light, and dry,
All your body's movement like
Thought in some more noble brain,
All your presence vivid as
The swords that whirled about you.
I know I shall remember
You for many, many years.
Your vision in my memory
Will teach and guide my vision,
Like the contemplation of
The deep heart of a jewel.

A letter from a flier,
'We came back up the Moselle
In the twilight, and I thought
Of your friend Ausonius. . . .'
Bright midnight, the Easter moon
Shepherds a sky of fleeces.
Reading, drinking Chateau Ausone,
I puzzle out those fluent pictures,
The footprints of Tu Fu grown old,
Hungry, lost on the Great West Road,
Dead, hostage of streams and rivers.
On the radio a piece
For the morticians, the Fauré
Requiem, sentimental,
Its themes remotely Japanese,
When they are not Gregorian;
And after it, a newscast,
The same story, fugitive,
Durable, as a torch of grass.
Paulinus and Bodhidharma,
The intact soul vanishes
In wildfire. Jungle or glacier,
The filth of the world strangles
One hundred million young men.
One hundred million men in arms!
More than lived in all Athens,
From beginning to end. Tonight,
The Feast of the Resurrection,
Easter, in a year of war,
The radio concert's choice
Is appropriate enough,
A sentimental Frenchman's
Ideas of death and rebirth,
The language of Roman ruin,

Of the fall of Jerusalem,
Tunes about cherry blossoms.
'Here alone in the night's heart,
In the midst of ten thousand sorrows,
I bribe the spring with wine.'

ADVENT

for Brother Antoninus

> *Rorate coeli, desuper, et nubes pluant
> justum. Aperiatur terra, et germinet
> Salvatorem.*

The year draws down. In the meadows
And high pastures, the green grass veins
The grey. Already the stubble
Fields are green. Orion stands
Another year over California,
Simple and lucent, guarding the full moon.
Dew descends from heaven
Good pours from the clouds.
The earth wavers on its whirling track.
We milk by lantern light. The shadows
Of the cattle are illimitable.
The lantern light knots in gouts of gold.
As the sun retreats, and the moon
Turns its face away and back again,
Following the spinning earth
Like our following lanterns
Through the dark, back to the white breath
Of the cattle, back to the smell
Of hay and dung and milk,
Back to the placental
Dark in the abandoned ruins,
God goes again to birth.

LUCRETIUS, III, 1053-1076

Baudelaire knew what it was like,
The typewriter keys red hot,
All the paint brushes a yard long,
The paint mixed with chewing gum.
I write letters and don't send them;
Dream away my poverty;
Make dozens of incredibly
Bad sketches; reread the great
Masterpieces; review my
Greek and Chinese, and discover
My vocabulary is gone;
Take my pulse; start out on walks,
And return home; my mind deep
And clear like the Deipnosophists.
Jean-Jacques, Amiel, Bashkirtsev,
It is possible to produce
A very influential
Ontology out of such
Material, of guaranteed
Ecumenical provenance.
Porch and Garden up to date,
Kierkegaard and Sacher-Masoch,
'One feels like a man about
To be executed.' Niebuhr
Discovers that everyone
Is his own Wanda Guillotine.
Liberal Protestantism
Goeth at last to its long home,
Only a few hours behind
The Capitalist System.
Die Ausrottung der Besten.
Just think, all the patronesses
Of the surrealistes feel
Like this all the time. In fact
Practically every female,
With an income, in our set does.

'In the cold autumn moonlight
The cicada dies by its shell.'
Even in jail, Mirabeau
Found work for idle hands to do.
The Rule of St. Benedict
Is very explicit about
The sickness that destroyeth
In the noonday.
                        One advantage
Of being learned, is that
There is no fix you can get in
Where you wont find company.
Even if your advisors
Cannot be called very helpful.

NO!

I have closed my ears, I refuse
To listen to my mouth weeping.
I have closed my mouth, I refuse
The taste of my weeping eyes.
I have closed my eyes on the past
As you want it remembered for
The rest of life, called 'forever'.
I was not there. I was away.
At the Poles, in the Amazon.
I am not going to have been
Where you say I was. You fancy
You can force me to have lived
The past you want. You are wrong.

A CHRISTMAS NOTE
FOR GERALDINE UDELL

Do the prairie flowers, the huge autumn
Moons, return in season?
Debs, Berkman, Larkin, Haywood, they are dead now.
All the girls are middle aged.
So much has escaped me, so much lies covert
In memory, and muffled
Like thunder muttering through sleep, that woke me,
To watch the city wink
Out in the violet light under the twisting rain.
Lightning storms are rare here,
In this statistically perfect climate.
The eucalyptus shed
Branches, doors banged, glass broke, the sea smashed its walls.
I, in my narrow bed,
Thought of other times, the hope filled post war years,
Exultant, dishevelled
Festivals, exultant eyes, dishevelled lips,
Eyes dulled now, and lips thinned,
Festivals that have betrayed their occasions.
I think of you in *Gas*,
The heroine on the eve of explosion;
Or angry, white, and still,
Arguing with me about Sasha's tragic book.
Here in the empty night,
I light the lamp and hunt for pad and pencil.
A million sleepers turn,
While bombs fall in their dreams. The storm goes away,
Muttering in the hills.
The veering wind brings the cold, organic smell
Of the flowing ocean.

STONE AND FLOWER

for Kathleen Raine

Here in America,
By the other ocean —
Your book, two years delayed —
In the spring evening.

I look from my window
Over a steep city,
From a hilltop higher
Than most of your England.

West of the dark mountains,
Over the white ocean,
That female planet burns,
Twisting in the green sky.

I think of you at work —
Against the apathy
Of war, all the squalor
Of ruin, your sure word:

Stone and flower moving
Each into the other
Their unmeasured cycles —
The perfume in the rock,

The fossilized pollen,
Phosphate in the petal,
The rose between the breasts,
The eyes' bag of diamonds.

My dear Kathleen, others
Have evoked a poet's
Responsibility,
And never raised a ghost

Out of the permanent
Wreckage of a world where
Wars are secret or not,
But never, never, stop.

Your poems give meaning to
The public tragedy
To which they lend themselves
On their own terms, as when

One sharp, six pointed star
Of snow falls from the black
Sky to the black water
And turns it all to ice.

GAMBLING

Thoughts of you spatter my thought.
Black drops fall from the sword edge
Of thunder. White cards scatter
Black and red equivocal
Hearts and spades. Death passes me
Daily and splashes her fierce
Chemicals in my hair. Clock
Ticks change voice and speak your name.
What a dish life is, with its
Sour grapes and broken glass.
I can remember your breasts,
That smell of marzipan.

TRANSLATIONS AND IMITATIONS

LEOPARDI: L'INFINITO

This lonely hill has always
Been dear to me, and this thicket
Which shuts out most of the final
Horizon from view. I sit here,
And gaze, and imagine
The interminable spaces
That stretch away, beyond my mind,
Their uncanny silences,
Their profound calms; and my heart
Is almost overwhelmed with dread.
And when the wind drones in the
Branches, I compare its sound
With that infinite silence;
And I think of eternity,
And the dead past, and the living
Present, and the sound of it;
And my thought drowns in immensity;
And shipwreck is sweet in such a sea.

From the Chinese

THE EMPEROR WU OF HAN

Majestic, from the most distant time,
The sun rises and sets.
Time passes and men cannot stop it.
The four seasons serve them,
But do not belong to them.
The years flow like water.
Everything passes away before my eyes.

Chilled by excess of passion,
Unsmiling, we drink farewell.
The candle, overcome by sorrow,
Weeps for us all through the night.

ANONYMOUS CHINESE

When Su was asked why his paintings
Were inexhaustibly suggestive,
He replied that he had prepared
Himself to see mountains and waters
In the stained walls of a prison cell.

SSU-MA KUANG

The yellow plums fatten
In the pouring rain.
Frogs sing in the marsh reeds.
Late into the night I wait,
Toying with the chessmen,
While the lamp wick reddens and falls.

ME

The bleeding hearts in the garden
Bloom early, but never fruit.
Every year they have spread further,
Underground, by creeping rootstocks.
Zeno's arrow in my heart,
I float in the plunging year.

THE LIGHT ON THE PEWTER DISH

Driving across the huge bridge
Above San Francisco Bay,
The United States Navy
Anchored, rank by deadly rank,
In the water under me,
And over me the sky filled
With hundreds of bombing planes,
My mind wandering idly,
I was suddenly aware
That Jacob Boehme flourished
During the Thirty Years' War.

ME AGAIN

They say I do not realize
The values of my own time.
What preposterous nonsense!
Ten years of wars, mountains of dead,
One hundred million armed men
And billions of paper dollars
Spent to disembowel mankind.
If they go on forever,
They will have realized less
Value than I can in one hour
Sitting at my typewriter.

ON A BEAUTIFUL BAR BUTTERFLY
IN THE BLACK CAT

Vinea submittit capr(e)as non semper edulis.
She-goats bred in vineyards are not always edible.

VALUE NEUTER

Traders, parsons, and stoolpigeons,
Always confuse value and price.
The long epistemological
Debauch of modern philosophy —
The police-professors mull over
Pilate's question. Judas consults
The best income tax attorneys.

DISCRIMINATION

I don't mind the human race.
I've got pretty used to them
In these past twenty-five years.
I don't mind if they sit next
To me on streetcars, or eat
In the same restaurants, if
It's not at the same table.
However, I don't approve
Of a woman I respect
Dancing with one of them. I've
Tried asking them to my home
Without success. I shouldn't
Care to see my own sister
Marry one. Even if she
Loved him, think of the children.
Their art is interesting,
But certainly barbarous.
I'm sure, if given a chance,
They'd kill us all in our beds.
And you must admit, they smell.

FACT

In the encyclopedia
Are facts on which you can't improve.
As: 'The clitoris is present
In all mammals. Sometimes, as in
The female hyena, it is
Very large.'

DE FERA DORMITA

Annos tres vesperi, passer venit, sub tecto
Vestibuli somno. Quid fecit bello Europa?
Annos tres, hieme aestateque, idem passer,
Capite velato, dormiens in tenebra glauca.

William Carlos Williams

BONAPARTISME

Napoleon on St. Helena
Read Homer. I am depressed
And read over my own manuscripts.
Pencilled on a list of books
And groceries I find two lines:
'High in the east a morrow soft and sweet.
This hour, this is our last hour glass.'
I no longer remember
If they are mine or another's.

FURTHER ADVANTAGES
OF LEARNING

One day in the Library,
Puzzled and distracted,
Leafing through a dull book,
I came on a picture
Of the vase containing
Buddha's relics. A chill
Passed over me. I was
Haunted by the touch of
A calm I cannot know,
The opening into that
Busy place of a better world.

UNDER SORACTE

Another day, deep in the stacks,
Where no one had come for years.
Walled in by the forbidding tomes
Of Migne's *Patrologia*,
I stood, reading the heart tearing
Plaints of Abelard. All at once
I realized that for some time
I had been smelling a sweet, light
Perfume, very faint, and very chic;
And then I heard the shiver
Of thin bracelets, and a murmur
That went on and paused and went on again;
And discovered that beyond me
In the next aisle a boy and girl
Made love in the most remote
Corner of knowledge.

THE DRAGON AND THE UNICORN

(1952)

"What is love?" said Pilate, and washed his hands.

ROSA MUNDI

Bright petals of evening
Shatter, fall, drift over Florence,
And flush your cheeks a redder
Rose and gleam like fiery flakes
In your eyes. All over Florence
The swallows whirl between the
Tall roofs, under the bridge arches,
Spiral in the zenith like larks,
Sweep low in crying clouds above
The brown river and the white
River bed. Your moist, quivering
Lips are like the wet scarlet wings
Of a reborn butterfly who
Trembles on the rose petal as
Life floods his strange body.
Turn to me. Part your lips. My dear,
Some day we will be dead.

I feel like Pascal often felt.

About the mid houre of the nicht

FIRE

The air is dizzy with swallows.

Sunset comes on the golden
Towers, on the Signoría.
In the Badía, the light goes
From the face of Filippino's
Weary lady, exhausted with
The devotion of her worshipper.
Across the face of the Duomo
The Campanile's blue shadow
Marks the mathematics of beauty.
In San Miniato the gold
Mosaics still glitter through
The smoky gloom. At the end

Of the Way of the Cross, the dense
Cypress wood, full of lovers,
Shivering with impatience.
As the dark thickens, two by two
They take each other. Nightfall, all
The wood is filled with soft moaning,
As though it were filled with doves.

LEDA HIDDEN

Christmas Eve, unseasonably cold,
I walk in Golden Gate Park.
The winter twilight thickens.
The park grows dusky before
The usual hour. The sky
Sinks close to the shadowy
Trees, and sky and trees mingle
In receding planes of vagueness.
The wet pebbles on the path
Wear little frills of ice like
Minute, transparent fungus.
Suddenly the air is full
Of snowflakes—cold, white, downy
Feathers that do not seem to
Come from the sky but crystallize
Out of the air. The snow is
Unendurably beautiful,
Falling in the breathless lake,
Floating in the yellow rushes.
I cannot feel the motion
Of the air, but it makes a sound
In the rushes, and the snow
Falling through their weaving blades

Makes another sound. I stand still,
Breathing as gently as I can,
And listen to these two sounds,
And watch the web of frail wavering
Motion until it is almost night.
I walk back along the lake path
Pure white with the new snow. Far out
Into the dusk the unmoving
Water is drinking the snow.
Out of the thicket of winter
Cattails, almost at my feet,
Thundering and stamping his wings,
A huge white swan plunges away.
He breaks out of the tangle,
And floats suspended on gloom.
Only his invisible
Black feet move in the cold water.
He floats away into the dark,
Until he is a white blur
Like a face lost in the night,
And then he is gone. All the world
Is quiet and motionless
Except for the fall and whisper
Of snow. There is nothing but night,
And the snow and the odor
Of the frosty water.

GOLDEN SECTION

Paestum of the twice blooming
Roses, the sea god's honey
Colored stone still strong against
The folly of the long decline
Of man. The snail climbs the Doric
Line, and the empty snail shell
Lies by the wild cyclamen.
The sandstone of the Roman
Road is marked with sun wrinkles
Of prehistoric beaches,
But no time at all has touched
The deep constant melodies
Of space as the columns swing
To the moving eye. The sea
Breathes like a drowsy woman.
The sun moves like a drowsy hand.
Poseidon's pillars have endured
All tempers of the sea and sun.
This is the order of the spheres,
The curve of the unwinding fern,
And the purple shell in the sea;
These are the spaces of the notes
Of every kind of music.
The world is made of number
And moved in order by love.
Mankind has risen to this point
And can only fall away,
As we can only turn homeward
Up Italy, through France, to life
Always pivoted on this place.

Finally the few tourists go,
The German photographers, the
Bevy of seminarians,
And we are left alone. We eat
In the pronaos towards the sea.
Greek food, small white loaves, smoked cheese,

Pickled squid, black figs, and honey
And olive oil, the common food
Of Naples, still, for those who eat.
An ancient dog, Odysseus' dog,
Spawned before there were breeds of dogs,
Appears, begs, eats, and disappears—
The exoteric proxy of
The god. And we too grow drowsy with
White wine, tarry from the wineskin.
The blue and gold shafts interweave
Across our nodding eyes. The sea
Prepares to take the sun. We go
Into the naos, open to the
Sky and make love, where the sea god
And the sea goddess, wet with sperm,
Coupled in the incense filled dark,
As the singing rose and was still.

Mist comes with the sunset. (The Yanks
Killed the mosquitoes.) Long lines of
Umber buffalo, their backs a
Rippling congruence, as in the
Paintings of Krishna, file across
The brilliant green sea meadows,
Under banners of white mist.
The fires of the bivouacs of
Spartacus twinkle in the hills.
Our train comes with the first stars.
Venus over the wine dark sea.

All the way back the train fills
And fills up, and fills again,
With girls from the fish canneries,
And girls from the lace factories,
And girls from the fields, who have been
Working twelve hours for nothing,
Or at the best a few pennies.
They laugh and sing, all the way
Back to Naples, like broad bottomed,
Deep bosomed angels, wet with sweat.

TIME SPIRALS

Under the second moon the
Salmon come, up Tomales
Bay, up Papermill Creek, up
The narrow gorge to their spawning
Beds in Devil's Gulch. Although
I expect them, I walk by the
Stream and hear them splashing and
Discover them each year with
A start. When they are frightened
They charge the shallows, their immense
Red and blue bodies thrashing
Out of the water over
The cobbles; undisturbed, they
Lie in the pools. The struggling
Males poise and dart and recoil.
The females lie quiet, pulsing
With birth. Soon all of them will
Be dead, their handsome bodies
Ragged and putrid, half the flesh
Battered away by their great
Lust. I sit for a long time
In the chilly sunlight by
The pool below my cabin
And think of my own life—so much
Wasted, so much lost, all the
Pain, all the deaths and dead ends,
So very little gained after
It all. Late in the night I
Come down for a drink. I hear
Them rushing at one another
In the dark. The surface of
The pool rocks. The half moon throbs
On the broken water. I
Touch the water. It is black,
Frosty. Frail blades of ice form

On the edges. In the cold
Night the stream flows away, out
Of the mountain, towards the bay,
Bound on its long recurrent
Cycle from the sky to the sea.

MIRROR

The afternoon ends with red
Patches of light on the leaves
On the northeast canyon wall.
My tame owl sits serenely
On his dead branch. A foolish
Jay squalls and plunges at him.
He is ignored. The owl yawns
And stretches his wings. The jay
Flies away screaming with fright.
My king snake lies in inert
Curves over books and papers.
Even his tongue is still, but
His yellow eyes are judicial.
The mice move delicately
In the walls. Beyond the hills
The moon is up, and the sky
Turns to crystal before it.
The canyon blurs in half light.
An invisible palace
Of glass, full of transparent
People, settles around me.
Over the dim waterfall
The intense promise of light
Grows above the canyon's cleft.
A nude girl enters my hut,
With white feet, and swaying hips,
And fragrant sex.

ONLY YEARS

I come back to the cottage in
Santa Monica Canyon where
Andrée and I were poor and
Happy together. Sometimes we
Were hungry and stole vegetables
From the neighbors' gardens.
Sometimes we went out and gathered
Cigarette butts by flashlight.
But we went swimming every day,
All year round. We had a dog
Called Proclus, a vast yellow
Mongrel, and a white cat named
Cyprian. We had our first
Joint art show, and they began
To publish my poems in Paris.
We worked under the low umbrella
Of the acacia in the dooryard.
Now I get out of the car
And stand before the house in the dusk.
The acacia blossoms powder the walk
With little pills of gold wool.
The odor is drowsy and thick
In the early evening.
The tree has grown twice as high
As the roof. Inside, an old man
And woman sit in the lamplight.
I go back and drive away
To Malibu Beach and sit
With a grey haired childhood friend and
Watch the full moon rise over the
Long rollers wrinkling the dark bay.

EMPTY MIRROR

As long as we are lost
In the world of purpose
We are not free. I sit
In my ten foot square hut.
The birds sing. The bees hum.
The leaves sway. The water
Murmurs over the rocks.
The canyon shuts me in.
If I moved, Basho's frog
Would splash in the pool.
All summer long the gold
Laurel leaves fell through space.
Today I was aware
Of a maple leaf floating
On the pool. In the night
I stare into the fire.
Once I saw fire cities,
Towns, palaces, wars,
Heroic adventures,
In the campfires of youth.
Now I see only fire.
My breath moves quietly.
The stars move overhead.
In the clear darkness
Only a small red glow
Is left in the ashes.
On the table lies a cast
Snake skin and an uncut stone.

DOUBLED MIRRORS

It is the dark of the moon.
Late at night, the end of summer,
The autumn constellations
Glow in the arid heaven.
The air smells of cattle, hay,
And dust. In the old orchard
The pears are ripe. The trees
Have sprouted from old rootstocks
And the fruit is inedible.
As I pass them I hear something
Rustling and grunting and turn
My light into the branches.
Two raccoons with acrid pear
Juice and saliva drooling
From their mouths stare back at me,
Their eyes deep sponges of light.
They know me and do not run
Away. Coming up the road
Through the black oak shadows, I
See ahead of me, glinting
Everywhere from the dusty
Gravel, tiny points of cold
Blue light, like the sparkle of
Iron snow. I suspect what it is,
And kneel to see. Under each
Pebble and oak leaf is a
Spider, her eyes shining at
Me with my reflected light
Across immeasurable distance.

IN DEFENSE OF THE EARTH

(1956)

For my daughters
Mary and Katharine

THE REFLECTING TREES
OF BEING AND NOT BEING

In my childhood when I first
Saw myself unfolded in
The triple mirrors, in my
Youth, when I pursued myself
Wandering on wandering
Nightbound roads like a roving
Masterless dog, when I met
Myself on sharp peaks of ice,
And tasted myself dissolved
In the lulling heavy sea,
In the talking night, in the
Spiraling stars, what did I
Know? What do I know now,
Of myself, of the others?
Blood flows out to the fleeing
Nebulae, and flows back, red
With all the worn space of space,
Old with all the time of time.
It is my blood. I cannot
Taste in it as it leaves me
More of myself than on its
Return. I can see in it
Trees of silence and fire.
In the mirrors on its waves
I can see faces. Mostly
They are your face. On its streams
I can see the soft moonlight
On the Canal du Midi.
I can see the leaf shadows
Of the plane trees on the deep
Fluids of your eyes, and the
Golden fires and lamps of years.

SHE IS AWAY

All night I lay awake beside you,
Leaning on my elbow, watching your
Sleeping face, that face whose purity
Never ceases to astonish me.
I could not sleep. But I did not want
Sleep nor miss it. Against my body,
Your body lay like a warm soft star.
How many nights I have waked and watched
You, in how many places. Who knows?
This night might be the last one of all.
As on so many nights, once more I
Drank from your sleeping flesh the deep still
Communion I am not always strong
Enough to take from you waking, the peace of love.
Foggy lights moved over the ceiling
Of our room, so like the rooms of France
And Italy, rooms of honeymoon,
And gave your face an ever changing
Speech, the secret communication
Of untellable love. I knew then,
As your secret spoke, my secret self,
The blind bird, hardly visible in
An endless web of lies. And I knew
The web too, its every knot and strand,
The hidden crippled bird, the terrible web.
Towards the end of night, as trucks rumbled
In the streets, you stirred, cuddled to me,
And spoke my name. Your voice was the voice
Of a girl who had never known loss
Of love, betrayal, mistrust, or lie.
And later you turned again and clutched
My hand and pressed it to your body.
Now I know surely and forever,
However much I have blotted our
Waking love, its memory is still
There. And I know the web, the net,

The blind and crippled bird. For then, for
One brief instant it was not blind, nor
Trapped, nor crippled. For one heart beat the
Heart was free and moved itself. O love,
I who am lost and damned with words,
Whose words are a business and an art,
I have no words. These words, this poem, this
Is all confusion and ignorance.
But I know that coached by your sweet heart,
My heart beat one free beat and sent
Through all my flesh the blood of truth.

MOCKING BIRDS

In mid-March in the heart of
The night, in the center of
The sterile city, in the
Midst of miles of asphalt and
Stone, alone and frustrated,
Wakeful on my narrow bed,
My brain spinning with worry,
There came to me, slipping through
The interstices of the
Blowing darkness, the living,
Almost imperceptible,
Faint, persistent, recurrent
Song of a single tree toad —
A voice sweeter than most birds.
Seven years ago we lay
Naked and moist, making love
Under the Easter full moon,
The thick fragrant light shaking
With the songs of mocking birds.

LONELINESS

To think of you surcharged with
Loneliness. To hear your voice
Over the recorder say,
"Loneliness." The word, the voice,
So full of it, and I, with
You away, so lost in it —
Lost in loneliness and pain.
Black and unendurable,
Thinking of you with every
Corpuscle of my flesh, in
Every instant of night
And day. O, my love, the times
We have forgotten love, and
Sat lonely beside each other.
We have eaten together,
Lonely behind our plates, we
Have hidden behind children,
We have slept together in
A lonely bed. Now my heart
Turns towards you, awake at last,
Penitent, lost in the last
Loneliness. Speak to me. Talk
To me. Break the black silence.
Speak of a tree full of leaves,
Of a flying bird, the new
Moon in the sunset, a poem,
A book, a person — all the
Casual healing speech
Of your resonant, quiet voice.
The word freedom. The word peace.

THE OLD SONG AND DANCE

You, because you love me, hold
Fast to me, caress me, be
Quiet and kind, comfort me
With stillness, say nothing at all.
You, because I love you, I
Am strong for you, I uphold
You. The water is alive
Around us. Living water
Runs in the cut earth between
Us. You, my bride, your voice speaks
Over the water to me.
Your hands, your solemn arms,
Cross the water and hold me.
Your body is beautiful.
It speaks across the water.
Bride, sweeter than honey, glad
Of heart, our hearts beat across
The bridge of our arms. Our speech
Is speech of joy in the night
Of gladness. Our words live.
Our words are children dancing
Forth from us like stars on water.
My bride, my well beloved,
Sweeter than honey, than ripe fruit,
Solemn, grave, a flying bird,
Hold me. Be quiet and kind.
I love you. Be good to me.
I am strong for you. I uphold
You. The dawn of ten thousand
Dawns is afire in the sky.
The water flows in the earth.
The children laugh in the air.

THE GREAT CANZON

Dante, Canzone 1

I have come at last to the short
Day and the long shadow when the
Hills turn white and the grass fades. Still
Longing stays green, stuck in this hard
Stone that speaks and hears as if it was
A woman. So it was this strange
Woman stood cold as shadowed snow,
Unmoved as stone by the sweet times
When the hills turn warm and turn from
White to green and are covered with
Flowers and grass. She, when she goes
Wreathed in herbs, drives every other
Woman from my mind — shimmering
Gold with green — so lovely that love
Comes to rest in her shadow, she
Who has caught me fast between
Two hills, faster far than fused stone.
No magic gem has her power.
No herb can heal her blow. I have
Fled through the fields, over the hills,
Trying to escape from such a
Woman, but there is no wall, no
Hill, no green leaf, can ever shade
Me from her light. Time was, I saw
Her dressed all in green, so lovely
She would have made a stone love her
As I do, who love her very
Shadow. Time was, we loved once in
The grass, she loving as ever
A woman was, and the high hills
Around us. But for sure rivers
Will flow back to the hills before
This wood, full of sap and green,
Ever catch fire again from me
As lovely women do — I who
Would be glad to sleep away my

Life turned to stone, or live on grass,
If only I could be where her
Skirts would cast their shadow on me.
Now when the shadow of the hills
Is blackest, under beautiful
Green, this young woman makes it
Vanish away at last, as if
She hid a stone in the grass.

GROWING

Who are you? Who am I? Haunted
By the dead, by the dead and the past and the
Falling inertia of unreal, dead
Men and things. Haunted by the threat
Of the impersonal, that which
Never will admit the person,
The closed world of things. Who are
You? Coming up out of the
Mineral earth, one pale leaf
Unlike any other unfolding,
And then another, strange, new,
Utterly different, nothing
I ever expected, growing
Up out of my warm heart's blood.
All new, all strange, all different.
Your own leaf pattern, your own
Flower and fruit, but fed from
One root, the root of our fused flesh.
I and thou, from the one to
The dual, from the dual
To the other, the wonderful,
Unending, unfathomable
Process of becoming each
Our selves for each other.

233

A LIVING PEARL

At sixteen I came West, riding
Freights on the Chicago, Milwaukee
And St. Paul, the Great Northern,
The Northern Pacific. I got
A job as helper to a man
Who gathered wild horses in the
Mass drives in the Okanogan
And Horse Heaven country. The best
We culled out as part profit from
The drive, the rest went for chicken
And dog feed. We took thirty head
Up the Methow, up the Twisp,
Across the headwaters of Lake
Chelan, down the Skagit to
The Puget Sound country. I
Did the cooking and camp work.
In a couple of weeks I
Could handle the stock pretty well.
Every day we saddled and rode
A new horse. Next day we put a
Packsaddle on him. By the
Time we reached Marblemount
We considered them well broken.
The scissorbills who bought them
Considered them untamed mustangs
Of the desert. In a few weeks
They were peacefully pulling
Milk wagons in Sedro-Wooley.
We made three trips a season
And did well enough for the
Post-war depression.
Tonight,
Thirty years later, I walk
Out of the deserted miner's
Cabin in Mono Pass, under
The full moon and the few large stars.

The sidehills are piebald with snow.
The midnight air is suffused
With moonlight. As Dante says,
"It is as though a cloud enclosed
Me, lucid, dense, solid, polished,
Like a diamond forged by the sun.
We entered the eternal pearl,
Which took us as water takes
A ray of light, itself uncleft."
Fifteen years ago, in this place,
I wrote a poem called "Toward
An Organic Philosophy."
Everything is still the same,
And it differs very little
From the first mountain pass I
Crossed so long ago with the
Pintos and zebra duns and
Gunmetal roans and buckskins,
And splattered lallapaloosas,
The stocky wild ponies whose
Ancestors came with Coronado.
There are no horse bells tonight,
Only the singing of frogs
In the snow-wet meadows, the shrill
Single bark of a mountain
Fox, high in the rocks where the
Wild sheep move silently through the
Crystal moonlight. The same feelings
Come back. Once more all the awe
Of a boy from the prairies where
Lanterns move through the comfortable
Dark, along a fence, through a field,
Home; all the thrill of youth
Suddenly come from the flat
Geometrical streets of
Chicago, into the illimitable
And inhuman waste places
Of the Far West, where the mind finds
Again the forms Pythagoras

Sought, the organic relations
Of stone and cloud and flower
And moving planet and falling
Water. Marthe and Mary sleep
In their down bags, cocoons of
Mutual love. Half my life has
Been passed in the West, much of it
On the ground beside lonely fires
Under the summer stars, and in
Cabins where the snow drifted through
The pines and over the roof.
I will not camp here as often
As I have before. Thirty years
Will never come for me again.
"Our campfire dies out in the
Lonely mountains. The transparent
Moonlight stretches a thousand miles.
The clear peace is without end."
My daughter's deep blue eyes sleep
In the moon shadow. Next week
She will be one year old.

FIFTY

Rainy skies, misty mountains,
The old year ended in storms.
The new year starts the same way.
All day, from far out at sea,
Long winged birds soared in the
Rushing sky. Midnight breaks with
Driving clouds and plunging moon,
Rare vasts of endless stars.
My fiftieth year has come.

THE LIGHTS IN THE SKY ARE STARS

for Mary

HALLEY'S COMET

When in your middle years
The great comet comes again
Remember me, a child,
Awake in the summer night,
Standing in my crib and
Watching that long-haired star
So many years ago.
Go out in the dark and see
Its plume over water
Dribbling on the liquid night,
And think that life and glory
Flickered on the rushing
Bloodstream for me once, and for
All who have gone before me,
Vessels of the billion-year-long
River that flows now in your veins.

THE GREAT NEBULA
OF ANDROMEDA

We get into camp after
Dark, high on an open ridge
Looking out over five thousand
Feet of mountains and mile
Beyond mile of valley and sea.
In the star-filled dark we cook
Our macaroni and eat
By lantern light. Stars cluster
Around our table like fireflies.
After supper we go straight
To bed. The night is windy
And clear. The moon is three days
Short of full. We lie in bed
And watch the stars and the turning

Moon through our little telescope.
Late at night the horses stumble
Around camp and I awake.
I lie on my elbow watching
Your beautiful sleeping face
Like a jewel in the moonlight.
If you are lucky and the
Nations let you, you will live
Far into the twenty-first
Century. I pick up the glass
And watch the Great Nebula
Of Andromeda swim like
A phosphorescent amoeba
Slowly around the Pole. Far
Away in distant cities
Fat-hearted men are planning
To murder you while you sleep.

THE HEART OF HERAKLES

Lying under the stars,
In the summer night,
Late, while the autumn
Constellations climb the sky,
As the Cluster of Hercules
Falls down the west
I put the telescope by
And watch Deneb
Move towards the zenith.
My body is asleep. Only
My eyes and brain are awake.
The stars stand around me
Like gold eyes. I can no longer
Tell where I begin and leave off.
The faint breeze in the dark pines,
And the invisible glass,
The tipping earth, the swarming stars
Have an eye that sees itself.

A MAZE OF SPARKS OF GOLD

Spring — the rain goes by, the stars
Shine pale beside the Easter
Moon. Scudding clouds, tossing leaves,
Whirl overhead. Blossoms fall
In the dark from the fragrant
Madroñe trees. You lie beside
Me, luminous and still in sleep.
Overhead bees sleep in their
Tree. Beyond them the bees in
The Beehive in the Crab drift
Slowly past, a maze of points
Of fire. I've had ten times your
Years. Time holds us both fixed fast
Under the bright wasting stars.

A SWORD IN A CLOUD OF LIGHT

Your hand in mine, we walk out
To watch the Christmas Eve crowds
On Fillmore Street, the Negro
District. The night is thick with
Frost. The people hurry, wreathed
In their smoky breaths. Before
The shop windows the children
Jump up and down with spangled
Eyes. Santa Clauses ring bells.
Cars stall and honk. Street cars clang.
Loud speakers on the lampposts
Sing carols, on juke boxes
In the bars Louis Armstrong
Plays *White Christmas*. In the joints
The girls strip and grind and bump
To *Jingle Bells*. Overhead
The neon signs scribble and
Erase and scribble again
Messages of avarice,

Joy, fear, hygiene, and the proud
Names of the middle classes.
The moon beams like a pudding.
We stop at the main corner
And look up, diagonally
Across, at the rising moon,
And the solemn, orderly
Vast winter constellations.
You say, "There's Orion!"
The most beautiful object
Either of us will ever
Know in the world or in life
Stands in the moonlit empty
Heavens, over the swarming
Men, women, and children, black
And white, joyous and greedy,
Evil and good, buyer and
Seller, master and victim,
Like some immense theorem,
Which, if once solved would forever
Solve the mystery and pain
Under the bells and spangles.
There he is, the man of the
Night before Christmas, spread out
On the sky like a true god
In whom it would only be
Necessary to believe
A little. I am fifty
And you are five. It would do
No good to say this and it
May do no good to write it.
Believe in Orion. Believe
In the night, the moon, the crowded
Earth. Believe in Christmas and
Birthdays and Easter rabbits.
Believe in all those fugitive
Compounds of nature, all doomed
To waste away and go out.
Always be true to these things.

They are all there is. Never
Give up this savage religion
For the blood-drenched civilized
Abstractions of the rascals
Who live by killing you and me.

PROTOPLASM OF LIGHT

How long ago
Frances and I took the subway
To Van Cortlandt Park. The people
All excited, small boys and
Cripples selling dark glasses.
We rushed to the open hills
North of the station as though
We'd be too late, and stood there
Hand in hand, waiting. Under
The trees the sun made little
Lunes of light through the bare branches
On the snow. The sky turned gray
And very empty. One by
One the stars came out. At last
The sun was only a thin
Crescent in our glasses with the
Bright planets nearby like watchers.
Then the great cold amoeba
Of crystal light sprang out
On the sky. The wind passed like
A silent crowd. The crowd sobbed
Like a passing wind. All the dogs
Howled. The silent protoplasm
Of light stood still in the black sky,
In its bowels, ringed with ruby
Fire, its stone-black nucleus.
Mercury, cold and dark like a
Fleck of iron, stood silent by it.
That was long ago.
Mary and I stand on the
Seashore and watch the sun sink

In the windy ocean. Layers
Of air break up the disc. It looks
Like a vast copper pagoda.
Spume blows past our faces, jellyfish
Pulse in the standing water,
Sprawl on the wet sand at our feet.
Twilight comes and all of the
Visible planets come out.
Venus first, and then Jupiter,
Mars and Saturn and finally
Mercury once more. Seals bark
On the rocks. I tell Mary
How Kepler never saw Mercury,
How, as he lay dying it shone
In his window, too late for him
To see. The mysterious
Cone of light leans up from the
Horizon into the pale sky.
I say, "Nobody knows what
It is or even where it is.
Maybe it is the great cloud
Of gas around the sun which
You will see some day if you
Are lucky. It stands out only
During an eclipse. I saw it
Long ago."

BLOOD ON A DEAD WORLD

A blowing night in late fall,
The moon rises with a nick
In it. All day Mary has
Been talking about the eclipse.
Every once in a while I
Go out and report on the
Progress of the earth's shadow.
When it is passing the half,
Marthe and Mary come out
And we stand on the corner

In the first wisps of chilling
Fog and watch the light go out.
Streamers of fog reach the moon,
But never quite cover it.
We have explained with an orange,
A grapefruit, and a lamp, not
That we expect a four
Year old child to understand —
Just as a sort of ritual
Duty. But we are surprised.
"The earth's shadow is like blood,"
She says. I tell her the Indians
Called an eclipse blood on the moon.
"Is it all the blood on the earth
Makes the shadow that color?"
She asks. I do not answer.

QUIETLY

Lying here quietly beside you,
My cheek against your firm, quiet thighs,
The calm music of Boccherini
Washing over us in the quiet,
As the sun leaves the housetops and goes
Out over the Pacific, quiet —
So quiet the sun moves beyond us,
So quiet as the sun always goes,
So quiet, our bodies, worn with the
Times and the penances of love, our
Brains curled, quiet in their shells, dormant,
Our hearts slow, quiet, reliable
In their interlocked rhythms, the pulse
In your thigh caressing my cheek. Quiet.

FOR ELI JACOBSON

December, 1952

There are few of us now, soon
There will be none. We were comrades
Together, we believed we
Would see with our own eyes the new
World where man was no longer
Wolf to man, but men and women
Were all brothers and lovers
Together. We will not see it.
We will not see it, none of us.
It is farther off than we thought.
In our young days we believed
That as we grew old and fell
Out of rank, new recruits, young
And with the wisdom of youth,
Would take our places and they
Surely would grow old in the
Golden Age. They have not come.
They will not come. There are not
Many of us left. Once we
Marched in closed ranks, today each
Of us fights off the enemy,
A lonely isolated guerrilla.
All this has happened before,
Many times. It does not matter.
We were comrades together.
Life was good for us. It is
Good to be brave — nothing is
Better. Food tastes better. Wine
Is more brilliant. Girls are more
Beautiful. The sky is bluer
For the brave — for the brave and
Happy comrades and for the
Lonely brave retreating warriors.
You had a good life. Even all
Its sorrows and defeats and

244

Disillusionments were good,
Met with courage and a gay heart.
You are gone and we are that
Much more alone. We are one fewer,
Soon we shall be none. We know now
We have failed for a long time.
And we do not care. We few will
Remember as long as we can,
Our children may remember,
Some day the world will remember.
Then they will say, "They lived in
The days of the good comrades.
It must have been wonderful
To have been alive then, though it
Is very beautiful now."
We will be remembered, all
Of us, always, by all men,
In the good days now so far away.
If the good days never come,
We will not know. We will not care.
Our lives were the best. We were the
Happiest men alive in our day.

ON A FLYLEAF OF RIME—
GASPARA STAMPA

Bought in the Libreria Serenissima
Venice, June 14, 1949

While the light of Canaletto
And Guardi turns to the light of
Turner, and the domes of the Saluta
Begin to take on the evening,
I drink chocolate and Vecchia
Romagna, that estimable
Brandy, on the terrace of
The Café International,
And read these twisting,
Burning pages. Love was
An agony for you, too, signora,
And came to no good end after
All the terrible price.
Enveloped in the evening
Sussura of this quiet city,
Where the loudest human sound
Is a footfall, I sit alone
With my own life. Last night I took
A gondola, out past the Giudecca,
Straight into the moonlight.
Coming back the monks
Were singing matins in San Giorgio
Maggiore. I wonder if it is possible
To be more alone than in a gondola
In Venice under the full moon
Of June. All I have for company
Are the two halves of my heart.

TIME IS THE MERCY
OF ETERNITY

Time is divided into
Seconds, minutes, hours, years,
And centuries. Take any
One of them and add up its
Content, all the world over.
One division contains much
The same as any other.
What can you say in a poem?
Past forty, you've said it all.
The dwarf black oak grows out of
The cliff below my feet. It
May be two hundred years old,
Yet its trunk is no bigger
Than my wrist, its crown does not
Come to my shoulder. The late
Afternoon sun behind it
Fills its leaves with light like
A gem tree, like the wishing
Tree of jewels in the Eastern
Stories. Below it the cliff
Falls sheer away five hundred
Feet to a single burnt pine,
And then another thousand
Feet to a river, noisy
In spate. Off beyond it stretches
Shimmering space, then fold on
Dimmer fold of wooded hills,
Then, hardly visible in
The pulsating heat, the flat
Lands of the San Joaquin Valley,
Boiling with life and trouble.
The pale new green leaves twinkle
In the rising air. A blue
Black, sharp-beaked, sharp-crested jay
Rests for a moment amongst

Them and then plunges off, down
Through the hazy June afternoon.
Far away the writhing city
Burns in a fire of transcendence
And commodities. The bowels
Of men are wrung between the poles
Of meaningless antithesis.
The holiness of the real
Is always there, accessible
In total immanence. The nodes
Of transcendence coagulate
In you, the experiencer,
And in the other, the lover.
When the first blooms come on the
Apple trees, and the spring moon
Swims in immeasurable
Clear deeps of palpable light,
I sit by the waterfall.
The owls call, one beyond the
Other, indefinitely
Away into the warm night.
The moist black rocks gleam faintly.
The curling moss smells of wet life.
The waterfall is a rope
Of music, a black and white
Spotted snake in the moonlit
Forest. The thighs of the goddess
Close me in. The moon lifts into
The cleft of the mountains and a
Cloud of light pours around me like
Blazing perfume. When the moon has
Passed on and the owls are loud in
My ears again, I kneel and drink
The cold, sweet, twisting water.

All day clouds drift up the canyon.
By noon the high peaks are hidden.
Thunder mutters in the distance.
Suddenly the canyon is gone.

My camp on its narrow ledge is
Isolated in swirling mist.
Even the nearby pines grow dim,
And recede into the grayness.
Yellow lightning bursts, like fire through
Smoke, and sets all the mist aglow.
Thunder explodes under my feet.
The rain pours hissing through the
Pine needles. White hailstones fall
Awry between the red pine trunks.
They rattle on my tent. I catch
Some and watch them melt in my hand.
As evening comes, birds ruffle
Their feathers, and fly gingerly
From branch to branch, and sing a few
Notes, while through the orange twilight
Fall green, widely spaced drops of rain.

For three days the clouds have piled up,
And rain has circled the mountains.
For a while it will fall over
Black Rock Pass, and then move across
To the red Kaweahs, and then
On to the white Whitney Range. But
Here by the lake it does not fall,
And the air grows more oppressive.
I swim lazily. Even the
Water seems to be heavier.
The air is full of mosquitoes.
After a listless lunch, I sit
On the bank reading the wise poems
Of Charles Cros. Suddenly the wind
Rises. The tent flaps noisily.
Twigs and dust and pine needles fly
In all directions. Then the wind
Drops and the rain falls on the lake.
The drops chime against the ripples
Like the Japanese glass wind bells
I loved so much as a child.

The rain is gone in an hour.
In the clear evening freshness,
I hear the bell on my donkey,
In his meadow, a mile away.
Nighthawks cry overhead and dive,
Thrumming their wings as they turn.
A deer comes down to the water.
The high passes are closed with snow.
I am the first person in this season.
No one comes by. I am alone
In the midst of a hundred mountains.

Five o'clock, mid-August evening,
The long sunlight is golden
On the deep green grass and bright
Red flowers of the meadow.
I stop where a meander
Of the brook forms a deep pool.
The water is greenish brown,
But perfectly transparent.
A small dense cloud of hundreds
Of midges, no bigger than
My head, hovers over it.
On the bank are two small frogs.
In the water are beetles,
Hydras, water bugs, larvae
Of several insects. On
The surface are water boatmen.
I realize that the color
Of the water itself is
Due to millions of active
Green flecks of life. It is like
Peering into an inkspot,
And finding yourself staring
Out into the Milky Way.
The deep reverberation
Of my identity with
All this plenitude of life
Leaves me shaken and giddy.

I step softly across the
Meadows as the deer lift their
Antlers and idly watch me.

Here on this high plateau where
No one ever comes, beside
This lake filled with mirrored mountains,
The hours and days and weeks
Go by without variation.
Even the rare storms pass over
And empty themselves on the peaks.
There are no fish in the water.
There are few deer or bear in the woods.
Only the bright blue damsel flies
On the reeds in the daytime,
And the nighthawks overhead
In the evening. Suspended
In absolutely transparent
Air and water and time, I
Take on a kind of crystalline
Being. In this translucent
Immense here and now, if ever,
The form of the person should be
Visible, its geometry,
Its crystallography, and
Its astronomy. The good
And evil of my history
Go by. I can see them and
Weigh them. They go first, with all
The other personal facts,
And sensations, and desires.
At last there is nothing left
But knowledge, itself a vast
Crystal encompassing the
Limitless crystal of air
And rock and water. And the
Two crystals are perfectly
Silent. There is nothing to
Say about them. Nothing at all.

A SINGING VOICE

Once, camping on a high bluff
Above the Fox River, when
I was about fourteen years
Old, on a full moonlit night
Crowded with whip-poor-wills and
Frogs, I lay awake long past
Midnight watching the moon move
Through the half drowned stars. Suddenly
I heard, far away on the warm
Air a high clear soprano,
Purer than the purest boy's
Voice, singing, "Tuck me to sleep
In my old 'Tucky home."
She was in an open car
Speeding along the winding
Dipping highway beneath me.
A few seconds later
An old touring car full of
Boys and girls rushed by under
Me, the soprano rising
Full and clear and now close by
I could hear the others singing
Softly behind her voice. Then
Rising and falling with the
Twisting road the song closed, soft
In the night. Over thirty
Years have gone by but I have
Never forgotten. Again
And again, driving on a
Lonely moonlit road, or waking
In a warm murmurous night,
I hear that voice singing that
Common song like an
Angelic memory.

OUR HOME IS IN THE ROCKS

for Richard Eberhart

Breasted, beginning his lectures,
"The development of religion
And thought in ancient Egypt" says,
"In going up to the daily
Task on some neighboring temple
In Nubia, I was not
Infrequently obliged to pass
Through the corner of a graveyard
Where the feet of a dead man,
Buried in a shallow grave
Were uncovered and extended
Directly across my path.
They were precisely like the rough
And calloused feet of the workmen
In our excavations. How old
The grave was I do not know, but
Anyone familiar with
The cemeteries of Egypt,
Ancient and modern, has found
Numerous bodies or portions
Of bodies, indefinitely
Old, which seemed about as well
Preserved as those of the living."

We went to call on a lady,
Whose father has seen the lifted
Ear of corn at Eleusis,
Her mother, a well tempered poetess,
Her brother was killed in Spain,
For his own epitaph he wrote,
"Thought shall be the harder,
Heart the keener,
Mood shall be the more
As our might lessens."
Hige sceal the heardra

Heorte the cenre
Mod sceal the mare
The ure maegan lythlath.
Which happens also to be the
Epigraph of Toynbee's sermon.
She too will be moderately immortal.

And now
I sit looking out of the cabin
At the rain falling through the green
Under-water gloom of the narrow
Gulch, listening to the counterpoint
Of rain and waterfall and leaf.
Somewhere in his wanderings
Today, my dog has rolled in
A spatched cock or flattened cat,
And the faint effluvium
Of dry death clings to his foolish
And frolicking body.

I think
Of Lucretius and Socrates
And the actor on the Titanic.
I suppose you can hear the leathery
Sibilant voice of death speaking
Behind their unbelievable
Plausibility.

Do I fear death?
As far as I can make out I
Feel towards death as Rochefoucauld
Must have felt, though I don't recall
He ever mentioned it.

The dead
Cow that stunk in the hemlock thicket
Three years ago is now only
Bright white bones on the bright green
Grass by day. When I walk out

Late at night they glimmer like pearls
By the waning moonlight, nodes of
Light in the amorphous dimness.
It is spring again and I am
Back from Europe. The frogs' children
Sing in the wet meadow. The green
Pronged fires burst from the buckeye
Again. Again the rosy web
Of alder twigs catches the moon.
Again the small hazel flowers
Put forth their crimson serpent tongues.
Perched on his rock the aplodontia,
The mountain beaver, with the face
Of an overfed angel, eyes me
With his black jewels of ultimate
Innocence. Of far feebler folk
Than the Scripture's coney, he dies
If touched, so quietly you can't
Believe he is dead, as he lies
So still in your hand, breathless, with
Dulling eyes.

XMAS COMING

November night. Waning moon
Cold after rain. Ferns of ice
Form on the puddles. Dead leaves
Are crisp with cold. Deer bound past,
Their eyes green in my lamplight.
The children grunt in their sleep.
Mary dreams of Christmas trees.
Baby Katharine of secrets,
The jolly secrets she can't tell.

MY HEART'S AS GAY
AS A YOUNG SUNFLOWER

Oh, who will shoe your pretty little foot,
    And who will glove your hand,
And who will kiss your cherry red lips,
    When I'm gone to the foreign land?

My pappy'll shoe my pretty little foot,
    And my mammy'll glove my hand,
And there's plenty of boys'll kiss my cherry red lips
    When you're gone to the foreign land.

Oh, who will comb your golden hair
    With the brand new turtle comb,
And who will kiss your satin neck,
    When I'm gone across the foam?

Oh, my sis will comb my golden hair,
    With the dark red turtle comb;
And I'll find them'll kiss my neck,
    Before ever you come home.

The doves fly off to the woods from the cote,
    But at night they all come home;
And my heart will turn like that to you,
    No matter how far I may roam.

Oh, the wild birds fly all day in the woods,
    From tree to tree they roam;
My heart's like the birds that have no cote,
    Wherever they roost is their home.

Oh, the crow is the bird with the blackest wing,
    And it turns to a purple hue;
If ever I loose this love that I hold,
    Let my body waste like the dew.

On top of the church is a bird that sits,
    And he turns with the winds as they blow;
My heart's not ready to hold to a man,
    So why do you plague me so?

My heart's as clear as a pane of glass,
    Your name's carved there in gold;
It'll stay right there till the day I die,
    For all men to behold.

THE MIRROR IN THE WOODS

A mirror hung on the broken
Walls of an old summer house
Deep in the dark woods. Nothing
Ever moved in it but the
Undersea shadows of ferns,
Rhododendrons and redwoods.
Moss covered the frame. One day
The gold and glue gave way and
The mirror slipped to the floor.
For many more years it stood
On the shattered boards. Once in
A long time a wood rat would
Pass it by without ever
Looking in. At last we came,
Breaking the sagging door and
Letting in a narrow wedge
Of sunlight. We took the mirror
Away and hung it in my
Daughter's room with a barre before
It. Now it reflects ronds, escartes,
Relevés and arabesques.
In the old house the shadows,
The wood rats and moss work unseen.

THE BAD OLD DAYS

The summer of nineteen eighteen
I read *The Jungle* and *The
Research Magnificent*. That fall
My father died and my aunt
Took me to Chicago to live.
The first thing I did was to take
A streetcar to the stockyards.
In the winter afternoon,
Gritty and fetid, I walked
Through the filthy snow, through the
Squalid streets, looking shyly
Into the people's faces,
Those who were home in the daytime.
Debauched and exhausted faces,
Starved and looted brains, faces
Like the faces in the senile
And insane wards of charity
Hospitals. Predatory
Faces of little children.
Then as the soiled twilight darkened,
Under the green gas lamps, and the
Sputtering purple arc lamps,
The faces of the men coming
Home from work, some still alive with
The last pulse of hope or courage,
Some sly and bitter, some smart and
Silly, most of them already
Broken and empty, no life,
Only blinding tiredness, worse
Than any tired animal.
The sour smells of a thousand
Suppers of fried potatoes and
Fried cabbage bled into the street.
I was giddy and sick, and out
Of my misery I felt rising
A terrible anger and out

Of the anger, an absolute vow.
Today the evil is clean
And prosperous, but it is
Everywhere, you don't have to
Take a streetcar to find it,
And it is the same evil.
And the misery, and the
Anger, and the vow are the same.

A DIALOGUE OF WATCHING

Let me celebrate you. I
Have never known anyone
More beautiful than you. I
Walking beside you, watching
You move beside me, watching
That still grace of hand and thigh,
Watching your face change with words
You do not say, watching your
Solemn eyes as they turn to me,
Or turn inward, full of knowing,
Slow or quick, watching your full
Lips part and smile or turn grave,
Watching your narrow waist, your
Proud buttocks in their grace, like
A sailing swan, an animal,
Free, your own, and never
To be subjugated, but
Abandoned, as I am to you,
Overhearing your perfect
Speech of motion, of love and
Trust and security as
You feed or play with our children.
I have never known any
One more beautiful than you.

MARY AND THE SEASONS

DRY AUTUMN

In the evening, just before
Sunset, while we were cooking
Supper, we heard dogs, high on
The west ridge, running a deer.
With unbelievable speed
They quartered down the hillside,
Crossed the gulch, climbed the east ridge
And circled back above us.
As they rushed down again, I
Ran to catch them. The barking
Stopped when they reached the creek bed.
As I came near I could hear
The last terrified bleating
Of a fawn. By the time I
Got there it was already dead.
When the dogs caught sight of me,
They scurried guiltily away.
The fawn was not torn. It had
Died of fear and exhaustion.

My dearest, although you are
Still too young to understand,
At this moment horrible
Black dogs with eyes of fire and
Long white teeth and slavering
Tongues are hunting you in the dark
Mountains to eat your tender heart.

SPRING RAIN

The smoke of our campfire lowers
And coagulates under
The redwoods, like low-lying
Clouds. Fine mist fills the air. Drops
Rattle down from all the leaves.

As the evening comes on
The treetops vanish in fog.
Two saw-whet owls utter their
Metallic sobbing cries high
Overhead. As it gets dark
The mist turns to rain. We are
All alone in the forest.
No one is near us for miles.
In the firelight mice scurry
Hunting crumbs. Tree toads cry like
Tiny owls. Deer snort in the
Underbrush. Their eyes are green
In the firelight like balls of
Foxfire. This morning I read
Mei Yao Chen's poems, all afternoon
We walked along the stream through
Woods and meadows full of June
Flowers. We chased frogs in the
Pools and played with newts and young
Grass snakes. I picked a wild rose
For your hair. You brought
New flowers for me to name.
Now it is night and our fire
Is a red throat open in
The profound blackness, full of
The throb and hiss of the rain.

AUTUMN RAIN

Two days ago the sky was
Full of mares' tails. Yesterday
Wind came, bringing low cigar
Shaped clouds. At midnight the rain
Began, the first fine, still rain
Of autumn. Before the rain
The night was warm, the sky hazy.
We lay in the field and watched
The glowing October stars,
Vega, Deneb, Altair, high,

Hercules and the Crown setting,
The Great Nebula distinct
Through the haze. Every owl
In the world called and made love
And scolded. Once in a while
We would see one on the sky,
Cruising, on wings more silent
Than silence itself, low over
The meadow. The air thickened.
The stars grew dim and went out.
The owls stopped crying in the wood.
Then the rain came, falling so
Gently on the tent we did
Not notice until a slight
Breeze blew it in on our faces.
At dawn it was still raining.
It cleared as we cooked breakfast.
We climbed through tatters of cloud
To the east ridge and walked through
The dripping, sparkling fir forest.
In the meadow at the summit
We ate lunch in the pale sun,
Ever so slightly cooler,
And watched the same long autumn
Mares' tails and came back down the
Steep rocks through the soaking ferns.

CLEAR AUTUMN

This small flat clearing is not
Much bigger than a large room
In the steep narrow canyon.
On every side the slender
Laurel trunks shut us in close.
High on the southern sidehill
Patches of sunlight filter
Through the fir trees. But the sun
Will not come back here until
Winter is past. New-fallen

Leaves shine like light on the floor.
The air hums with low-flying
Insects, too weakened to rise.
The stream has stopped. Underground,
A trickle seeps from pool to pool.
All the summer birds have gone.
Only woodpeckers and jays
And juncos have stayed behind.
Soon the rains will start, and then
Fine, silent, varied thrushes
Will come from the dark rain forests
Of the Northwest, but not yet.
We climb to the long west ridge
That looks out on the ocean
And eat lunch at a high spring
Under the rocks at the top.
Holstein calves cluster around
And watch us impassively.
No wind moves in the dry grass.
The sky and the distant sea,
The yellow hills, stretching away,
Seem seen in a clouded mirror.
Buzzards on the rising air
Float without moving a wing.
Jet bombers play at killing
So high overhead only
Long white scrawls can be seen, the
Graffiti of genocide.
The planes are invisible.
Away from the sun the air
Glitters with millions of glass
Needles, falling from the zenith.
It is as though oxygen
And nitrogen were being
Penetrated and replaced
By some shining chemical.
It is the silk of a swarm
Of ballooning spiders, flashes
Of tinsel and drifting crystal

In the vast rising autumn air.
When we get back everything
Is linked with everything else
By fine bright strands of spun glass,
The golden floor of October,
Brilliant under a gauze of light.

SNOW

Low clouds hang on the mountain.
The forest is filled with fog.
A short distance away the
Giant trees recede and grow
Dim. Two hundred paces and
They are invisible. All
Day the fog curdles and drifts.
The cries of the birds are loud.
They sound frightened and cold. Hour
By hour it grows colder.
Just before sunset the clouds
Drop down the mountainside. Long
Shreds and tatters of fog flow
Swiftly away between the
Trees. Now the valley below
Is filled with clouds like clotted
Cream and over them the sun
Sets, yellow in a sky full
Of purple feathers. After dark
A wind rises and breaks branches
From the trees and howls in the
Treetops and then suddenly
Is still. Late at night I wake
And look out of the tent. The
Clouds are rushing across the
Sky and through them is tumbling
The thin waning moon. Later
All is quiet except for
A faint whispering. I look
Out. Great flakes of wet snow are

Falling. Snowflakes are falling
Into the dark flames of the
Dying fire. In the morning the
Pine boughs are sagging with snow,
And the dogwood blossoms are
Frozen, and the tender young
Purple and citron oak leaves.

ANOTHER TWILIGHT

Far out across the Great Valley
The sun sets behind the Coast Range.
The distant mountains mingle
With the haze of the valley,
Purple folded into purple.
Over them the evening
Turns orange and green, the white fire
Of Venus and the transparent
Crescent moon. Venus is caught
In the Crab's claws, the moon creeps
Between the Virgin's open thighs.
Bats dodge and squeak between the trees.
A velvety, chocolate-colored
Bear comes and begs for food. Two
Gray and orange foxes quarter
Over the ground below camp,
Searching for scraps. Their cubs
Peek out from the manzanita.

THE ORPHIC SOUL

As I walk slowly along
The sun flecked wood road, a large
Fritillary comes to rest
On my naked shoulder, then
Flies in a little spiral
And comes back again and
Again to my shoulders and
Arms, fluttering over me
Like the souls on Orphic tombs.
This never happened to me
Before, and I feel my flesh
Has suddenly become sweet
With a metamorphosis
Kept secret even from myself.

HUMAN, AVIAN,
VEGETABLE, BLOOD

Today, three days before Christmas,
I had planned to cut some berries
From the toyon bush in the yard.
For three years it has not done well.
This is the first year it produced
A decent crop. But this morning
A flock of thirty migrating
Robins appeared, and before noon
Every berry had been eaten.
This year we will buy our foliage
As usual, and the symbols
Of incarnate flesh we tended
All year will be flying, mingled
With pale hot bird blood, high over
The barren Mexican mountains.

THOU SHALT NOT KILL

A Memorial for Dylan Thomas

I

They are murdering all the young men.
For half a century now, every day,
They have hunted them down and killed them.
They are killing them now.
At this minute, all over the world,
They are killing the young men.
They know ten thousand ways to kill them.
Every year they invent new ones.
In the jungles of Africa,
In the marshes of Asia,
In the deserts of Asia,
In the slave pens of Siberia,
In the slums of Europe,
In the nightclubs of America,
The murderers are at work.

They are stoning Stephen,
They are casting him forth from every city in the world.
Under the Welcome sign,
Under the Rotary emblem,
On the highway in the suburbs,
His body lies under the hurling stones.
He was full of faith and power.
He did great wonders among the people.
They could not stand against his wisdom.
They could not bear the spirit with which he spoke.
He cried out in the name
Of the tabernacle of witness in the wilderness.
They were cut to the heart.
They gnashed against him with their teeth.
They cried out with a loud voice.
They stopped their ears.

They ran on him with one accord.
They cast him out of the city and stoned him.
The witnesses laid down their clothes
At the feet of a man whose name was your name —
You.

You are the murderer.
You are killing the young men.
You are broiling Lawrence on his gridiron.
When you demanded he divulge
The hidden treasures of the spirit,
He showed you the poor.
You set your heart against him.
You seized him and bound him with rage.
You roasted him on a slow fire.
His fat dripped and spurted in the flame.
The smell was sweet to your nose.
He cried out,
"I am cooked on this side,
Turn me over and eat,
You
Eat of my flesh."

You are murdering the young men.
You are shooting Sebastian with arrows.
He kept the faithful steadfast under persecution.
First you shot him with arrows.
Then you beat him with rods.
Then you threw him in a sewer.
You fear nothing more than courage.
You who turn away your eyes
At the bravery of the young men.

You,
The hyena with polished face and bow tie,
In the office of a billion dollar
Corporation devoted to service;
The vulture dripping with carrion,
Carefully and carelessly robed in imported tweeds,

Lecturing on the Age of Abundance;
The jackal in double-breasted gabardine,
Barking by remote control,
In the United Nations;
The vampire bat seated at the couch head,
Notebook in hand, toying with his decerebrator;
The autonomous, ambulatory cancer,
The Superego in a thousand uniforms;
You, the finger man of behemoth,
The murderer of the young men.

II

What happened to Robinson,
Who used to stagger down Eighth Street,
Dizzy with solitary gin?
Where is Masters, who crouched in
His law office for ruinous decades?
Where is Leonard who thought he was
A locomotive? And Lindsay,
Wise as a dove, innocent
As a serpent, where is he?
     Timor mortis conturbat me.

What became of Jim Oppenheim?
Lola Ridge alone in an
Icy furnished room? Orrick Johns,
Hopping into the surf on his
One leg? Elinor Wylie
Who leaped like Kierkegaard?
Sara Teasdale, where is she?
     Timor mortis conturbat me.

Where is George Sterling, that tame fawn?
Phelps Putnam who stole away?
Jack Wheelwright who couldn't cross the bridge?
Donald Evans with his cane and
Monocle, where is he?
     Timor mortis conturbat me.

John Gould Fletcher who could not
Unbreak his powerful heart?
Bodenheim butchered in stinking
Squalor? Edna Millay who took
Her last straight whiskey? Genevieve
Who loved so much; where is she?
     Timor mortis conturbat me.

Harry who didn't care at all?
Hart who went back to the sea?
     Timor mortis conturbat me.

Where is Sol Funaroff?
What happened to Potamkin?
Isidor Schneider? Claude McKay?
Countee Cullen? Clarence Weinstock?
Who animates their corpses today?
     Timor mortis conturbat me.

Where is Ezra, that noisy man?
Where is Larsson whose poems were prayers?
Where is Charles Snider, that gentle
Bitter boy? Carnevali,
What became of him?
Carol who was so beautiful, where is she?
     Timor mortis conturbat me.

III

Was their end noble and tragic,
Like the mask of a tyrant?
Like Agamemnon's secret golden face?
Indeed it was not. Up all night
In the fo'c'sle, bemused and beaten,
Bleeding at the rectum, in his
Pocket a review by the one
Colleague he respected, "If he
Really means what these poems
Pretend to say, he has only

270

One way out —." Into the
Hot acrid Caribbean sun,
Into the acrid, transparent,
Smoky sea. Or another, lice in his
Armpits and crotch, garbage littered
On the floor, gray greasy rags on
The bed. "I killed them because they
Were dirty, stinking Communists.
I should get a medal." Again,
Another, Simenon foretold,
His end at a glance. "I dare you
To pull the trigger." She shut her eyes
And spilled gin over her dress.
The pistol wobbled in his hand.
It took them hours to die.
Another threw herself downstairs,
And broke her back. It took her years.
Two put their heads under water
In the bath and filled their lungs.
Another threw himself under
The traffic of a crowded bridge.
Another, drunk, jumped from a
Balcony and broke her neck.
Another soaked herself in
Gasoline and ran blazing
Into the street and lived on
In custody. One made love
Only once with a beggar woman.
He died years later of syphilis
Of the brain and spine. Fifteen
Years of pain and poverty,
While his mind leaked away.
One tried three times in twenty years
To drown himself. The last time
He succeeded. One turned on the gas
When she had no more food, no more
Money, and only half a lung.
One went up to Harlem, took on
Thirty men, came home and

Cut her throat. One sat up all night
Talking to H. L. Mencken and
Drowned himself in the morning.
How many stopped writing at thirty?
How many went to work for *Time?*
How many died of prefrontal
Lobotomies in the Communist Party?
How many are lost in the back wards
Of provincial madhouses?
How many on the advice of
Their psychoanalysts, decided
A business career was best after all?
How many are hopeless alcoholics?
René Crevel!
Jacques Rigaud!
Antonin Artaud!
Mayakofsky!
Essenin!
Robert Desnos!
Saint Pol Roux!
Max Jacob!
All over the world
The same disembodied hand
Strikes us down.
Here is a mountain of death.
A hill of heads like the Khans piled up.
The first-born of a century
Slaughtered by Herod.
Three generations of infants
Stuffed down the maw of Moloch.

IV

He is dead.
The bird of Rhiannon.
He is dead.
In the winter of the heart.
He is Dead.
In the canyons of death,

They found him dumb at last,
In the blizzard of lies.
He never spoke again.
He died.
He is dead.
In their antiseptic hands,
He is dead.
The little spellbinder of Cader Idris.
He is dead.
The sparrow of Cardiff.
He is dead.
The canary of Swansea.
Who killed him?
Who killed the bright-headed bird?
You did, you son of a bitch.
You drowned him in your cocktail brain.
He fell down and died in your synthetic heart.
You killed him,
Oppenheimer the Million-Killer,
You killed him,
Einstein the Gray Eminence.
You killed him,
Havanahavana, with your Nobel Prize.
You killed him, General,
Through the proper channels.
You strangled him, Le Mouton,
With your *mains étendues.*
He confessed in open court to a pince-nezed skull.
You shot him in the back of the head
As he stumbled in the last cellar.
You killed him,
Benign Lady on the postage stamp.
He was found dead at a Liberal Weekly luncheon.
He was found dead on the cutting room floor.
He was found dead at a *Time* policy conference.
Henry Luce killed him with a telegram to the Pope.
Mademoiselle strangled him with a padded brassiere.
Old Possum sprinkled him with a tea ball.
After the wolves were done, the vaticides

Crawled off with his bowels to their classrooms
   and quarterlies.
When the news came over the radio
You personally rose up shouting, "Give us Barabbas!"
In your lonely crowd you swept over him.
Your custom-built brogans and your ballet slippers
Pummeled him to death in the gritty street.
You hit him with an album of Hindemith.
You stabbed him with stainless steel by Isamu Noguchi,
He is dead.
He is Dead.
Like Ignacio the bullfighter,
At four o'clock in the afternoon.
At precisely four o'clock.
I too do not want to hear it.
I too do not want to know it.
I want to run into the street,
Shouting, "Remember Vanzetti!"
I want to pour gasoline down your chimneys.
I want to blow up your galleries.
I want to burn down your editorial offices.
I want to slit the bellies of your frigid women.
I want to sink your sailboats and launches.
I want to strangle your children at their finger paintings.
I want to poison your Afghans and poodles.
He is dead, the little drunken cherub.
He is dead,
The effulgent tub thumper.
He is Dead.
The ever living birds are not singing
To the head of Bran.
The sea birds are still
Over Bardsey of Ten Thousand Saints.
The underground men are not singing
On their way to work.
There is a smell of blood
In the smell of the turf smoke.
They have struck him down,
The son of David ap Gwilym.

They have murdered him,
The Baby of Taliessin.
There he lies dead,
By the Iceberg of the United Nations.
There he lies sandbagged,
At the foot of the Statue of Liberty.
The Gulf Stream smells of blood
As it breaks on the sand of Iona
And the blue rocks of Canarvon.
And all the birds of the deep sea rise up
Over the luxury liners and scream,
"You killed him! You killed him.
In your God damned Brooks Brothers suit,
You son of a bitch."

THE AMERICAN CENTURY

Blackbirds whistle over the young
Willow leaves, pale celadon green,
In the cleft of the emerald hills.
My daughter is twenty-one months old.
Already she knows the names of
Many birds and flowers and all
The animals of barnyard and zoo.
She paddles in the stream, chasing
Tiny bright green frogs. She wants
To catch them and kiss them. Now she
Runs to me with a tuft of rose
Gray owl's clover. "What's that? Oh! What's that?"
She hoots like an owl and caresses
The flower when I tell her its name.
Overhead in the deep sky
Of May Day jet bombers cut long
White slashes of smoke. The blackbird
Sings and the baby laughs, midway
In the century of horror.

A BESTIARY

for my daughters, Mary and Katharine

Aardvark

The man who found the aardvark
Was laughed out of the meeting
Of the Dutch Academy.
Nobody would believe him.
The aardvark had its revenge —
It returned in dreams, in smoke,
In anonymous letters.
One day somebody found out
It was in Hieronymus
Bosch all the time. From there it
Had sneaked off to Africa.

Ant

Achilles, Aesop, Mark Twain,
Stalin, went to the ant.
Your odds are one to three if
You decide to ignore it.
The aardvark, he eats them up,
And frightens all the people.

Bear

When the world is white with snow,
The bear sleeps in his darkness.
When the people are asleep,
The bear comes with glowing eyes
And steals their bacon and eggs.
He can follow the bees from
Point to point for their honey.
The bees sting but he never
Pays them any attention.

Tame bears in zoos beg for buns.
Two philosophies of life:
Honey is better for you
Than buns; but zoo tricks are cute
And make everybody laugh.

Cat

There are too many poems
About cats. Beware of cat
Lovers, they have a hidden
Frustration somewhere and will
Stick you with it if they can.

Coney

Coneys are a feeble folk,
But their home is in the rocks.
If you've only got one rock
There are better things to do
With it than make a home of it.

Cow

The contented cow gives milk.
When they ask, "Do you give milk?"
As they surely will, say "No."

Deer

Deer are gentle and graceful
And they have beautiful eyes.
They hurt no one but themselves,
The males, and only for love.
Men have invented several
Thousand ways of killing them.

Eagle

The eagle is very proud.
He stays alone, by himself,
Up in the top of the sky.
Only brave men find his home.
Few telescopes are sharper
Than his eyes. I think it's fine
To be proud, but remember
That all the rest goes with it.
There is another kind of
Eagle on flags and money.

Fox

The fox is very clever.
In England people dress up
Like a movie star's servants
And chase the fox on horses.
Rather, they let dogs chase him,
And they come along behind.
When the dogs have torn the fox
To pieces they rub his blood
On the faces of young girls.
If you are clever do not
Let anybody know it,
But especially Englishmen.

Goat

G stands for goat and also
For genius. If you are one,
Learn from the other, for he
Combines domestication,
Venery, and independence.

Herring

The herring is prolific.
There are plenty of herrings.
Some herrings are eaten raw.
Many are dried and pickled.
But most are used for manure.
See if you can apply this
To your history lessons.

Horse

It is fun to ride the horse.
If you give him some sugar
He will love you. But even
The best horses kick sometimes.
A rag blowing in the wind
Can cause him to kill you. These
Characteristics he shares
With the body politic.

I

Take care of this. It's all there is.
You will never get another.

Jackal

The jackal's name is often
Used as a term of contempt.
This is because he follows
The lion around and lives
On the leavings of his kill.
Lions terrify most men
Who buy meat at the butcher's.

Kangaroo

As you know, the kangaroo
Has a pocket, but all she
Puts in it is her baby.
Never keep a purse if all
You can find to put in it
Is additional expense.
(The reception of these words
Will also serve to warn you:
NEVER MAKE FUN OF BABIES!)

Lion

The lion is called the king
Of beasts. Nowadays there are
Almost as many lions
In cages as out of them.
If offered a crown, refuse.

Man

Someday, if you are lucky,
You'll each have one for your own.
Try it before you pick it.
Some kinds are made of soybeans.
Give it lots to eat and sleep.
Treat it nicely and it will
Always do just what you want.

Mantis

In South Africa, among
The Bushmen, the mantis is
A god. A predatory
And cannibalistic bug,
But one of the nicer gods.

Monkey

Monkeys are our relatives.
On observing their habits
Some are ashamed of monkeys,
Some deny the relation,
Some are ashamed of themselves.
They throw coconuts at us.

N

N is for nothing. There is
Much more of it than something.

Okapi

The okapi is extinct.
The reason is under "N."

Possum

When in danger the possum
Plays dead. The state when dying
Plays danger. With the possum
This trick works; sometimes
He escapes. But when the state
Plays with death, it really dies.

Quagga

The quagga is extinct also.
If it hadn't been for the quagga
We'd be short a beast for "q."
I can't think of one, can you?

Raccoon

The raccoon wears a black mask,
And he washes everything
Before he eats it. If you
Give him a cube of sugar,
He'll wash it away and weep.
Some of life's sweetest pleasures
Can be enjoyed only if
You don't mind a little dirt.
Here a false face won't help you.

Scarecrow

A hex was put on you at birth.
Society certified your
Existence and claimed you as
A citizen. Don't let it
Scare you. Learn to cope with a world
Which is built entirely of fake,
And in which, if you find a truth
Instead of a lie, it is due
To somebody's oversight.
These stuffed old rags are harmless,
Unless you show them the fear
Which they can never warrant,
Or reveal the contempt which
Of course is all they deserve.
If you do, they'll come to life,
And do their best to kill you.

Seal

The seal when in the water
Is a slippery customer
To catch. But when he makes love
He goes on dry land and men
Kill him with clubs.
To have a happy love life,
Control your environment.

Trout

The trout is taken when he
Bites an artificial fly.
Confronted with fraud, keep your
Mouth shut and don't volunteer.

Uncle Sam

Like the unicorn, Uncle
Sam is what is called a myth.
Plato wrote a book which is
An occult conspiracy
Of gentlemen pederasts.
In it he said ideas
Are more nobly real than
Reality, and that myths
Help keep people in their place.
Since you will never become,
Under any circumstances,
Gentlemen pederasts, you'd
Best leave these blood-soaked notions
To those who find them useful.

Unicorn

The unicorn is supposed
To seek a virgin, lay
His head in her lap, and weep,
Whereupon she steals his horn.
Virginity is what is
Known as a privation. It is
Very difficult to find
Any justification for
Something that doesn't exist.
However, in your young days
You might meet a unicorn.
There are not many better
Things than a unicorn horn.

Vulture

St. Thomas Aquinas thought
That vultures were lesbians
And fertilized by the wind.
If you seek the facts of life,
Papist intellectuals
Can be very misleading.

Wolf

Never believe all you hear.
Wolves are not as bad as lambs.
I've been a wolf all my life,
And have two lovely daughters
To show for it, while I could
Tell you sickening tales of
Lambs who got their just deserts.

You

Let Y stand for you who says,
"Very clever, but surely
These were not written for your
Children?" Let Y stand for yes.

Zebra

Clothes do not make the zebra.
Better wear a convict's stripes
Free on the lonely savannah
Than the panoplied harness
Of a queen on Rotten Row,
Or a thief's colors at Ascot.

MOTHER GOOSE

Do not pick my rosemary.
Do not pick my rue.
I am saving up my sorrow,
And I have none for you.

I expect to meet a lover
Who will break my heart.
He will be a nobleman.
His folks will make us part.

When my heart is broken
I will jump in the sea.
You can take the herbs of sorrow
And throw them after me.

Hidden in the briar bush
The ogre masturbates.
High in her tower,
The lady sits and waits.
She sends him an apple
By her little foot page.
He cannot eat the apple
For a heart sick with rage.
Here come the posse
And set the bush on fire.
The lady in the tower
Knows she is a liar.
Take the ogre's ashes,
Cast them in the sea.
There they will mingle
With a billion ladies' pee.

Last night I saw in the moon
Three little rabbits
Eating a prune.
Pipe in the mouth,
Glass in the hand,
Listening to the music
Of Dead Men's Band.
Missus, Mister,
Have some wine!
No thank you, bunnies,
I'll drink mine.

A gold and silver bird
Is flying in the meadow.
Gold and silver scissors
Are cutting in the shadow.
Come home and eat your clabber.
Your mother cries, "Come home!"
Mice have dabbled in your clabber,
These two hours gone.
Come home! Come home!

I came into the kitchen.
Death was cooking meat.
I sneaked up behind him,
And seized his hands and feet.
I held him up above me,
And threw him in the stew.
The sun turned yellow,
The sky turned blue.
The pot boiled over.
The stove blew up.
Death escaped up the chimney,

And left just a cup.
I drank the cup down quickly,
And now I'll never die.
But there'll be no yellow sun
And no more blue sky.

This is the way we plant our feet.
A la mode. Deep. Deep. Deep.
This is the way we plant our hands.
A la mode. Damned. Damned. Damned.
This is the way we plant our hearts.
A la mode. Smart. Smart. Smart.
This is the way we plant our heads.
A la mode. Dead. Dead. Dead.

Disemboweled babies
Drift in the sky.
Exploded mothers
Waft gently by.
Hear all the voices
Give a mighty shout
When the fathers find out
They are wrong side out.

Once there was a nightingale
Sang above their bed.
A jolly nightingale,
The night they were wed.
A nightingale of ashes.
The nightingale is dead.

A nightingale of dust.
The nightingale is dead.
And the world turns away.
The world turns,
And echoes in the head.

Hide the white stone
In the left fist.
Hide the white stone
In the right fist.
I am your secret brother.
Where is the white stone?
You've swallowed it.
You dirty bastard.

Jeanette Brunette
Had a wooden leg.
Her mother beat her,
And set her to beg.
She begged for meat,
She begged for bread.
They gave her swine's feet
And a spoiled cabbage head.
She begged for gold.
They gave her a nail.
The nail made her bold.
She hid it in a pail.
When her mother was asleep
She drove it in her head.
She didn't cry a bit
When her mother lay dead.

An old faggot who's lost his class,
A gray-haired valet with a sagging ass,
Hanging on the well rope,
Without love, faith, or hope.
Put pansies and lilies in a mustard pot
On his unkempt grave. Forget the old sot.

Ram. Damn. Slicker Sam,
Stole the crown
And away he ran.
The bishops cursed.
The generals swore.
Sam gave the crown
To his hot whore.
The ladies wept.
The lords all cried.
The queen slept
By Sam's side.

Diane de Poitiers, Josephine and Pompadour
Were doing something ugly all over the floor.
In came a white kitten with a green skull,
Said, "Ladies, don't you know we are all in Hell?"

This is the gallows that hung the maid.
This is the carpenter
Who built the gallows
That hung the maid.
These are the dogs
Who tore the carpenter

Who built the gallows
That hung the maid.
This is the hangman
Who bought the dogs
Who tore the carpenter
Who built the gallows
That hung the maid.
This is the gold
That paid the hangman
Who bought the dogs
Who tore the carpenter
Who built the gallows
That hung the maid.
This is the prince
Who gave the gold
That paid the hangman
Who bought the dogs
Who tore the carpenter
Who built the gallows
That hung the maid.
This is the maid
Who loved the prince
Who gave the gold
That paid the hangman
Who bought the dogs
That tore the carpenter
Who built the gallows
That hung the maid.
This is the carpenter
Who loved the maid
Who loved the prince
Who gave the gold
That paid the hangman
Who bought the dogs
That tore the carpenter
Who built the gallows
That hung the maid.

Marborough went to the war.
Cavendish stayed to home.
Marborough died of a pox,
Cavendish of a bomb.
Serves the stinkers jolly well right.

The heart is bitten.
The bone is broken.
The words are written.
The curse is spoken.
The cannibal frogs,
With bloody jaws,
Climb the blazing logs,
And write the laws.

Ibbitty, Bibbitty, Sibbitty, Sab.
Ibbitty, Bibbitty, Kanaba.
The Queen's name is Mad Mab.
The King's name is Baba.

Ibbitty, Bibbitty, Sibbitty, Sab.
Ibbitty, Bibitty, Kanaba.
Where is the knave in the taxi cab,
Who kidnapped our King Baba?

Ibbitty, Bibbitty, Sibbitty, Sab.
Ibbitty, Bibbitty, Kanaba.
Into the bloody ditch with Mab!
We've fried the liver of Baba!

Ibbitty, Bibbitty, Sibbitty, Sab.
Ibbitty, Bibbitty, Kanaba.
The King's name is Fat Dab.
The Queen's name is Raba.

The red wind blew.
The black wind blew.
At last there blew the blue.
Said the last naked devil
To the last naked angel,
"Girl, I think we're through."

EPIGRAMS AND TRANSLATIONS

ON A MILITARY GRAVEYARD

Stranger, when you come to Washington
Tell them that we lie here
Obedient to their orders.

After Simonides

SURVIVAL OF THE FITTEST

I realize as I
Cast out over the lake
At thirteen thousand feet —
I don't know where you are.
It has been years since we
Married and had children
By people neither of
Us knew in the old days.
But I still catch fish with flies
Made from your blonde pubic hair.

REVOLT

Outside of the movies
I have seen a monocle
On the eye of a living man
Only three times in my life,
On a Hollywood producer,
On a German officer,
And on a speaker at the
London Anarchist Group.

AFTER SAPPHO

I loved you, Leslie, long ago,
In the flower of your youth,
When I was just an ungainly boy.

LOST ETC.

The expatriates of the
Twenties and their leader Pound
Were those who, in an age of
World revolt found nothing more
Important to revolt against
Than the Eighteenth Amendment.

NEATNESS IS ALL

Out of Ptolemy's principle
Of economy and Occam's
Razor have come all the great
Omnivorous, rectangular
Immortal cosmophages.

SENSE OF PROPORTION

The old lion hunter and I
Exchange good-bys. "See you again
Someday in the woods." The last
Time I saw him was on the
Santa Lucia Ridge in
Nineteen twenty-nine. It isn't
Likely. He is seventy-three
And I am forty-eight. Someday
Will never come round again.

A BREAD AND BUTTER LETTER

Although it was not my home
The first cold plum blossom by
The window smelled just the same.

METEMPSYCHOSIS

Two months old, already
Across my daughter's face
Pass faces long past and dead.

ON THE POST OFFICE

Have you ever forgotten
The first time, in the evil
Boiling cauldron of New York,
You saw, high in the carven stone,
That noble sentence of
Herodotus?

AFTER SA'ADI

I said, "I do not fear the
Day when we shall part, I shall
Be strong." But when the day came,
Strength failed me.

FACT

Chirotherium tracks occur
Mainly in the Middle Bunter.

FROM THE PERSIAN

Naked out of the dark we came.
Naked into the dark we go.
Come to my arms, naked in the dark.

ILLUSION

When we were young, because we
Were older than the heroes
And heroines of fiction,
We thought we were middle-aged.

FROM THE PERSIAN

You are like the moon except
For your dark hair. You are like
Venus, except for your lips,
Crimson and perfumed, and like
The sun except that you are
Most splendid naked, at night.

VALUTA

Have you ever noticed how, the
World over, fairy princesses
Delight to give themselves to louts
And cowherds whom they enrich past
Belief? With all the privilege
And wealth of fairy land, the hot
Sweat of mortality gives off
A warmth more precious than all the
Illimitable bounties of
Deathlessness.

. . . . lives in the woods,
Where she languidly enjoys
A dim-witted lover, Nature,
Endemetriosis,
Exophthalmia, marasmus,
Too much money. She has moments
She Does Things With Her Hands, Lovely
Things, with an exquisite sense of
Chic. I saw her last at cocktails
In her town studio in
1937. Everybody
Was there, e.g., all the leading
Fairies and/or WPA
Officials. The smell of tweeds,
Blue Boar, and carbon paper
Was overpowering. The din
Of Phi Beta Kappa keys
Was deafening. There were an
Indeterminate number
Of spaniels pissing on their
Masters' Scotch brogans, and on
Other people's shoes. They were
Drinking the boys on the Ebro
Out of the trenches by Christmas.
A novelist who had been
In Spain spoke. Recently I hear
She has been entertaining
The leading male whore of Paris,
France, that pimp with the face of a
Poisoned Irish setter, who has
Been had by all the sexes of
Six continents. They say he has
Converted her to Anarchism,
A fascinating new theory
Which is sweeping England, and
Is the rage with all the really
Rafinée modistes and parfumistes.
Isn't that exciting?
KEEP OFF MY BANDWAGON YOU SOW!

PORTRAIT OF THE AUTHOR AS
A YOUNG ANARCHIST

1917-18-19,
While things were going on in Europe,
Our most used term of scorn or abuse
Was "bushwa." We employed it correctly,
But we thought it was French for "bullshit."
I lived in Toledo, Ohio,
On Delaware Avenue, the line
Between the rich and poor neighborhoods.
We played in the jungles by Ten Mile Creek,
And along the golf course in Ottawa Park.
There were two classes of kids, and they
Had nothing in common: the rich kids
Who worked as caddies, and the poor kids
Who snitched golf balls. I belonged to the
Saving group of exceptionalists
Who, after dark, and on rainy days,
Stole out and shat in the golf holes.

AFTER THE ANTHOLOGY

Artemis, more passionate
Than Aphrodite, at sunset
Your light rose in the east, and
All night was a fire in
The trees over us. Now alone
You hang, pale and splendid above
The dim sea while the first glow
Runs round the fringe of the mountains.
Go and inflame the pulses
Of the stolid Chinese. Leave us
To sleep exhausted till you return.

All day I hoe weeds.
All night I sleep.
All night I hoe again
In dreams the weeds of the day.

Anonymous

Did a cuckoo cry?
I open the door
And look about.
There is only the moon
Alone in the night.

Anonymous

In the summer, by the river,
Let us sit in the evening
Watching the lights of the boats
Caught and confused
In a net of fireflies.

Anonymous

In the open sea
With the thousand birds
Crying around me,
How can I ever give up
The life of a sailor?

Anonymous

The first time I saw you
Was last year in May,
In May, bathing in a pool
Crowded with iris.

When I look at her
Asleep in the dawn,
The body of my girl
Is like a lily in
The field of May.

The cicada cries out,
Burning with love.
The firefly burns
With silent love.

When I went with you to your ship
To say good-by,
My tears choked me
And I said nothing.

The sound of my laughter
Awoke me from the dream
Where we lay together,
And I looked around me,
My eyes filled with tears.

Anonymous

The nightingale on the flowering plum,
The stag beneath the autumn maple,
And you and me together in bed,
Happy as two fish in the water.

Anonymous

The snow falls and falls.
The mountains and meadows sleep.
Only an old mill
Stays awake.

Anonymous

He is so young
He will not find the road.
Angel of death,
I will pay you
To carry him on your shoulders.

Anonymous

I will remember forever
How I met you all alone,
Your dead white face
Gleaming like foxfire
In the rainy midnight.

Anonymous

Out of doors, I think,
At home I think,
How she looked that day
As she went by
Trailing the skirts of
Her crimson dress.

Anonymous

The plovers cry
Over the evening waves
Of Lake Omi.
In my withering heart
I remember the past.

Kakinomoto no Hitomaro

When I gathered flowers
For my girl
From the top of the plum tree,
The lower branches
Drenched me with dew.

Kakinomoto no Hitomaro

302

In the Spring garden,
In the colored shadow
Of peach blossoms,
A girl stands
On a white path.

Otomo no Yakamochi

Under the autumn moon
The fading chrysanthemums
Look like transparent crystals.

Anonymous

A hundred thousand birds
Warble in the Spring.
All things are made new.
I alone
Grow old and pass.

Anonymous

I wait and he does not come.
What difference does it make
If the nightingale sings,
When the flowering branch
Is broken?

Anonymous

I went out in the Spring
To gather the young herbs.
So many petals were falling,
Drifting in confused flight,
That I lost my way.

Ki no Tsurayuki

Wing by wing the wild geese fly,
Silhouetted so clearly
Against high white clouds
That I can count them
All the autumn night,
Under the moon.

Anonymous

I am so lost
In the black depths
Of the nights of love
That I can no longer tell
Dream from reality.

Ariwara no Narihira

Is my hair beginning to change color
That was once blacker than berries?
Or have snowflakes fallen
On my mirror?

Anonymous

Long after the moon had set,
But before cockcrow,
The drake was driven
From his lonely covert
By the mating of the wild geese.

Anonymous

Although the drake fled
Out into the starlit haze
Of the autumn morning,
He longs to return
To the down-lined nest
Of the young wild duck.

Anonymous

Setting sun,
Drifting clouds,
New moon,
Evening twilight,
What do they matter to me?

Ishikawa Takuboku

I do not know why
But it is as though
There were a cliff
Inside my head
From which, every day,
Clods of earth fall.

Ishikawa Takuboku

I picked up my mother
In play. But when I lifted
That frail light body,
I was so overcome
I could not take three steps.

Ishikawa Takuboku

In the passing summer
I send you chrysanthemums
And asters for your birthday,
A flower bridge between us,
As we stand equidistant
Across life's solstice.

Anonymous

FIVE TANKA BY AKIKO NO YOSANO

I

Once, far over the breakers,
I caught a glimpse
Of a white bird
And fell in love
With this dream which obsesses me.

II

Swifter than hail,
Lighter than a feather,
A vague sorrow
Crossed my mind.

III

The nightingale has not come
To sing on this misty day.
Somewhere, I guess, he is sleeping,
His jeweled claws neatly doubled.

IV

Left on the beach
Full of water,
A worn-out boat
Reflects the white sky
Of early autumn.

V

Over the old honeymoon cottage
At the mountain temple
The wild cherry blossoms are falling.
Here, in the desolate false dawn,
The stars go out in heaven.

———————

All the hot night
The quail
Sleepless in his cage.

Masaoka Shiki

The wild geese cry.
Below them on the reefs
The waves
White in the night.

Masaoka Shiki

Frozen in the ice
A maple leaf.

Masaoka Shiki

On the eve of death
The autumn cicada
Is noisier than ever.

Masaoka Shiki

Fresh from the void
The moon
On the waves of the sea.

Masaoka Shiki

Shitting in the winter turnip field,
The distant lights of the city.

Masaoka Shiki

Winter midnight,
My voice does not
Sound like my own.

Otsuji

SAND

Slow-footed, in the blaze of noon,
I walk along a white sandy path.
Over the distant roofs a red flag
Droops in the windless air.
The fields are barren,
The tumbledown buildings
Bake in the heat.
Fruit spilled on the bricks
Rots and stinks.
In the midsummer fields
The white sandy path
Breaks off and begins again,
In the midday terror
All is still,
No one moves.

Kitahara Hakushu

When I am old and infirm
I fear I shall no longer
Be able to roam among
The beautiful mountains.
Clarifying my mind,
I shall meditate on mountain
Trails which wander in vision.

Tsung Ping

My dear, what have you done
With our old red kite?
Let's fly it again this evening
As high as we can,
Through the driving sleet
Towards the moon in the sky.

The shore is far away now
Where we were young together once.
The red kite is torn and battered,
But maybe it will still fly.

My dear, come, let's fly it wildly,
As far out as we can
With all the cords of the heart
Through the falling sleet
Towards the moon in the sky.

Saijo Yaso

I did not want you, Candida.
I did not ask you to come.
You eat your heart? My heart
Eats me. I did not want you,
Candida. You came anyway.

Anonymous Latin

The muddy rat in the muddy rice field
Lives stuck in the mud.
It is because of myself, it is
My own fault life disgusts me.

I called up the sun, "Hello, Sun?"
The peach-colored sun
Hardly answered.
The telephone operator is as deaf
As she is surly.

The wires are crossed,
The line is busy,
Life is always like this.

On the mountain peaks the moon shines.
The world is tranquil in the silver night.
The muddy rat in the muddy rice field
Sleeps with his mate in his arms.

Horiguchi Daigaku

THEY SAY THIS ISN'T A POEM

I

All that is is a harmony,
Otherwise it would not endure.
Harmony of the parts with the whole
Is the definition of goodness.
Therefore all that is is good.
Man is part of all that is, so
He is part of its harmony.
Therefore he is by nature good.
Insofar as he knows what is,
He knows it because he is
Within himself a harmony
Of parts in a whole, of the same
Kind as all that is. Therefore,
The harmony of all that is
Without man can unite with
The harmony of all that is
Within man as a knowable
Good, an inner moral good.
But if this good is known within
By one party, man, it must
Also be known by the other
Party, All That Is, hence he who
Is in perfect accord with All
That Is can act upon It
Without effort, with a kind
Of reciprocity, like acts
Of the mutual love of friends.
How beautiful and specious
And how stinking with the blood
Of wars and crucifixions.

II

The order of the universe
Is only a reflection
Of the human will and reason.
All being is contingent,
No being is self-subsistent.
All objects are moved by others.
No object moves itself.
All beings are caused by others.
No being is its own cause.
There is no perfect being.
Being has no economy.
Entities are multiplied
Without necessity. They
Have no sufficient reason.
The only order of nature
Is the orderly relation
Of one person to another.
Non-personal relations
Are by nature chaotic.
Personal relations are
The pattern through which we see
Nature as systematic.
Homer, and all sensible
Men since, have told us again
And again, the universe —
The great principles and forces
That move the world — have order
Only as a reflection
Of the courage, loyalty,
Love, and honesty of men.
By themselves they are cruel
And utterly frivolous.
The man who yields to them goes mad,
Kills his child, his wife or friend
And dies in the bloody dust,
Having destroyed the treasured
Labor of other men's hands.
He who outwits them survives
To grow old in his own home.

CODICIL

Most of the world's poetry
Is artifice, construction.
No one reads it but scholars.
After a generation
It has grown so overcooked,
It cannot be digested.
There is little I haven't
Read, and dreary stuff it was.
Lamartine—Gower—Tasso—
Or the metaphysicals
Of Cambridge, ancient or modern,
And their American apes.
Of course for years the ruling
Class of English poetry
Has held that that is just what
Poetry is, impersonal
Construction, where personal
Pronouns are never permitted.
If rigorously enough
Applied, such a theory
Produces in practice its
Opposite. The poetry
Of Eliot and Valery,
Like that of Pope, isn't just
Personal, it is intense,
Subjective revery as
Intimate and revealing,
Embarrassing if you will,
As the indiscretions of
The psychoanalyst's couch.
There is always sufficient
Reason for a horror of
The use of the pronoun, "I."

NATURAL NUMBERS

(1964)

For my daughters
Mary and Katharine

There is a square for every
Natural number. If we
Divide the squares into even
And odd, we find that we can
Place the natural numbers
And the two sets of even
And odd squares in one to one
Correspondence.
            We will never
Run out of squares. But neither
Will we run out of even
Or odd squares. Rest assured, though
Squares are inexhaustible, and
Problems concerning squares are
Also inexhaustible,
So are natural numbers.

HOMER IN BASIC

Glitter of Nausicaä's
Embroideries, flashing arms,
And heavy hung maiden hair;
Doing the laundry, the wind
Brisk in the bright air
Of the Mediterranean day.
Odysseus, hollow cheeked,
Wild eyed, bursts from the bushes.
Mary sits by the falling
Water reading Homer while
I fish for mottled brook trout
In the sun mottled riffles.
They are small and elusive.
The stream is almost fished out.
Water falls through shimmering
Panelled light between the red
Sequoias, over granite
And limestone, under green ferns
And purple lupin. Time was
I caught huge old trout in these
Pools and eddies. These are three
Years old at the very most.
Mary is seven. Homer
Is her favorite author.
It took me a lifetime of
Shames and wastes to understand
Homer. She says, "Aren't those gods
Terrible? All they do is
Fight like those angels in Milton,
And play tricks on the poor Greeks
And Trojans. I like Aias
And Odysseus best. They are
Lots better than those silly
Gods." Like the ability
To paint, she will probably
Outgrow this wisdom. It too
Will wither away as she

Matures and a whole lifetime
Will be spent getting it back.
Now she teaches Katharine
The profound wisdom of seven
And Katharine responds with
The profound nonsense of three.
Grey haired in granite mountains,
I catch baby fish. Ten fish,
And Homer, and two little
Girls pose for a picture by
The twenty foot wide, cinnamon
Red trunk of a sequoia.
As I snap the camera,
It occurs to me that this
Tree was as big as the pines
Of Olympos, not just before
Homer sang, but before Troy
Ever fell or Odysseus
Ever sailed from home.

FISH PEDDLER AND COBBLER

Always for thirty years now
I am in the mountains in
August. For thirty Augusts
Your ghosts have stood up over
The mountains. That was nineteen
Twenty seven. Now it is
Nineteen fifty seven. Once
More after thirty years I
Am back in the mountains of
Youth, back in the Gros Ventres,
The broad park-like valleys and
The tremendous cubical
Peaks of the Rockies. I learned
To shave hereabouts, working
As cookee and night wrangler.

Nineteen twenty two, the years
Of revolutionary
Hope that came to an end as
The iron fist began to close.
No one electrocuted me.
Nothing happened. Time passed.
Something invisible was gone.
We thought then that we were the men
Of the years of the great change,
That we were the forerunners
Of the normal life of mankind.
We thought that soon all things would
Be changed, not just economic
And social relationships, but
Painting, poetry, music, dance,
Architecture, even the food
We ate and the clothes we wore
Would be ennobled. It will take
Longer than we expected.
These mountains are unchanged since
I was a boy wandering
Over the West, picking up
Odd jobs. If anything they are
Wilder. A moose cow blunders
Into camp. Beavers slap their tails
On their sedgy pond as we fish
From on top of their lodge in the
Twilight. The horses feed on bright grass
In meadows full of purple gentian,
And stumble through silver dew
In the full moonlight.
The fish taste of meadow water.
In the morning on far grass ridges
Above the red rim rock wild sheep
Bound like rubber balls over the
Horizon as the noise of camp
Begins. I catch and saddle
Mary's little golden horse,
And pack the first Decker saddles
I've seen in thirty years. Even

The horse bells have a different sound
From the ones in California.
Canada jays fight over
The last scraps of our pancakes.
On the long sandy pass we ride
Through fields of lavender primrose
While lightning explodes around us.
For lunch Mary catches a two pound
Grayling in the whispering river.
No fourteen thousand foot peaks
Are named Sacco and Vanzetti.
Not yet. The clothes I wear
Are as unchanged as the Decker
Saddles on the pack horses.
America grows rich on the threat of death.
Nobody bothers anarchists anymore.
Coming back we lay over
In Ogden for ten hours.
The courthouse square was full
Of miners and lumberjacks and
Harvest hands and gandy dancers
With broken hands and broken
Faces sleeping off cheap wine drunks
In the scorching heat, while tired
Savage eyed whores paraded the street.

PROUST'S MADELEINE

Somebody has given my
Baby daughter a box of
Old poker chips to play with.
Today she hands me one while
I am sitting with my tired
Brain at my desk. It is red.
On it is a picture of
An elk's head and the letters
B.P.O.E.—a chip from

A small town Elks' Club. I flip
It idly in the air and
Catch it and do a coin trick
To amuse my little girl.
Suddenly everything slips aside.
I see my father
Doing the very same thing,
Whistling "Beautiful Dreamer,"
His breath smelling richly
Of whiskey and cigars. I can
Hear him coming home drunk
From the Elks' Club in Elkhart
Indiana, bumping the
Chairs in the dark. I can see
Him dying of cirrhosis
Of the liver and stomach
Ulcers and pneumonia,
Or, as he said on his deathbed, of
Crooked cards and straight whiskey,
Slow horses and fast women.

Poems at L'Atelier, Route Tholonet,

AIX EN PROVENCE

AUTUMN

The children have colds and snore
In the night. The rain falls on
All autumn Provence, the gold
And orange and green and purple
Hidden in rustling darkness.
At my feet under the stove
Pierre Lapin sleeps and purrs.
I open the door and walk
Down the garden path towards
The ghostly statue of Flora.
Behind the clouds the moon is full.

The night is like a sea cave
At noon, and a wet owl flies
By me, silent as a fish.
The wind is shifting, the pines
On the opposite hill have
Begun to murmur like water.
Here it is still except for
The slow sweep of massive rain.
Heavy rain soaked gold leaves drop
From the plane trees through the dark.

CHRISTMAS

The biggest tree in Provence.
A milky faïence barber's bowl.
A merde d'oie velvet waistcoat.
Medieval poetry.
A most bouffant cretonne skirt.
A merde d'oie sweater. A mantilla.
Six copper pots. A brass nameplate.
Dolls. A crèche with santons.
Boules. Nine-pins. Dresses. Dozens
Of packages from the States.
A goose with prunes and almonds.
Champagne, Chateau Simon, cognac.
Outside the ruts are frozen.
Cézanne's pines are steely gray.
Mont Sainte Victoire is not blue
Or lavender in the sky,
It is pure bright limestone gray.
It is two weeks since the sound
Of the mines at Gardanne came
Over the hill on the South wind.
The girls sing songs from "Mireille"
And the "Pastourelle Maurel,"
And act out the parts, turn about.
Pierre Lapin purrs under
The smoky poêle. A cloud
Of frost hangs under the bare
Plane trees on Cour Mirabeau.
We drink grog in the Deux Garçons.

We visit two friends from the States.
We visit a heroine
Of the Resistance. At Mass,
As the Bishop passed our row,
He gave his ring to our girls
To kiss. But the professors
And the Gaullist intellectuals
Still snub us on the street.
We visit the bazaar for
The home for the aged infirm.
On the festooned arch it says,
"Les souvenirs des jours
Heureux sont terribles
A ceux qui souffrent
Et qui sont seuls."
Midnight, the Spring stars rise up
Over Mont Sainte Victoire standing
Like a crystal of smoky quartz
In the sky at the road's end.

SPRING

There are no images here
In the solitude, only
The night and its stars which are
Relationships rather than
Images. Shifting darkness,
Strains of feeling, lines of force,
Webs of thoughts, no images,
Only night and time aging
The night in its darkness, just
Motion in space in the dark.
It is a night full of darkness,
And space, and stars, and the hours
Going by, and time going by,
And the night growing old, and all
The webs, and nets, of relationships
Changing, and it is Spring night
In Provence, here where I am,
And under the half moon the almond
Buds are ready to burst. Before noon

The blossoms will open, here by
This peach colored house amongst
The steel gray pines and the gray
Limestone cliffs. Now the buds
Are round and tight in the dim
Moonlight, in the night that
Stretches on forever, that had
No beginning, and that will
Never end, and it doesn't mean
Anything. It isn't an image of
Something. It isn't a symbol of
Something else. It is just an
Almond tree, in the night, by
The house, in the woods, by
A vineyard, under the setting
Half moon, in Provence, in the
Beginning of another Spring.

SPRING

In the morning all the almond trees
Are blooming all over Provence like
They were blooming in a popular song.
Everywhere in the uplands in the woods
Where the old trees have shattered the
Ancient walls, everywhere by the pale
Ochre ruined houses, the almond trees
Are blooming. In the dry bright February,
All day I walk in the lifeless forest.
Nothing moves. Once in a great while
Some magpies rustle and cry, off in the
Trees somewhere. Once in a great while
I smell a hidden polecat or a deserted
Badger hole. Every few hundred meters,
There is a high wall of dry laid stone,
Stretching away out of sight through
The forest, fencing ruin from ruin.
Roofless houses, broken walls, dry
Canals, roads that go nowhere now. Even
The shooting blinds are abandoned.
Everywhere there are almond trees

Just out in bloom this morning,
And black jagged dead olives
With silver green shoots coming
Up around them. No sound. Only
The movement of leaves and stones.

SPRING

Wind in almond blossoms.
Ants on limestone mountains.
Cézanne's bones in red earth.
Countless vines on red earth.
Black wine on oak tables.
They drink love or hate as
The old plane trees blossom.
They drink coffee or pastis
Under the blowing young leaves.
Under feathery pines,
On red and grey hillsides,
Hidden from the mistral,
Two by two they make love.
In red sand pits, squad by squad,
Soldiers shoot at paper men.

ON THE EVE OF THE PLEBISCITE

The Mistral blows, the plane leaves
Parachute to earth. The Cour
Mirabeau turns from submarine
Green to blue grey and old gold.
When the wind drops it is warm
And drowsy. Glace or pastis
In a sunny chair, the Aixois
Decline to winter. Civic
Calm, the contemplative heart
Of Mediterranean
Civilization throbs with
Its slow, all governing pulse.
Tricolor posters, surcharged
OUI or NON flicker and battle
Like broken film on the screen

Of a malodorous cinema.
The Jeunesse Dorée of the
Law School hunt a sensitive
Overcivilized Algerian
Fellow student between the
Parked cars, around the plane trees,
Like an exhausted fox.
Horror tightens its steel bands
On this land and on every
Heart. Lewd sycophancy and
Brutalized indifference
Rule the highbrow terrasses
And the once militant slums.
Clowns and torturers and cheap
Literary adventurers
Parade like obscene dolls. This
Is no country I ever knew.
And who tightens the screws?
And who pulls these puppets' wires?
Oh, how well I remember
Listening to Chancellor
Bruening's last appeal. Late night,
By the cold green eye of the short-
Wave radio. "You have raised up
Forces from the bottom of
Society. You think they
Will be your willing tools. I
Tell you they will betray you
And destroy you. I beseech
You, bethink yourselves before
It is too late." To whom did
He speak? To the State Department,
The Foreign Office, National City,
Chase, The Bank of England,
Shell, Standard Oil, Krupp, US Steel,
Vickers, Dupont, the same ones
Who are still there—"reducing the heart
Of Europe to the status of a barbaric
Colony." And behind them—to you
By whose indifferent consent they rule.

Young, in Spring, I gathered
Flowers on the mountain.
Old, in Autumn, I pick
Sedges by the river.
Positive—negative.
Negative—positive.
Ordinary people
Never understand me.
As long as I have lovely
Children I have nothing
To be sorry about.

Geese out of Sweden cry,
Going past in the night.
Under the yellowing
Plane trees, over the walled
Pond, the swallows circle
For the last times. They swarm,
High in the bright Fall air
In the evenings. Then
One day they are all gone.
The great leaves float down like
Golden crumpled letters,
Fill the pond and cover the
Avenue in Cézanne's village.
On warm days ballooning
Spiders fill the air with
Threads and spicules of light.

Spring comes back. Trees blossom
In order: almond, plum,
Cherry, peach, last, apple.
Green gold maple tassles,
Rosy alder, yellow
Poplar catkins, and then
Great pompoms of chestnuts,

White and rose. One day
One swallow flies above
Flooded river meadows.
Next week they are all back.

Winter, children learn the stars.
Spring, children gather wild
Jonquils, violets, orchids.

Springs and Autumns gone by
I know by their record,
But I can no longer
Keep track of them
In my own memory.

My girls are eight and four.
Their hearts beat systole
And diastole. Their young
Legs twinkle in the deep
Meadow amongst flowers.

Poems at Casa San Rafaelle, Monte Berico,

VICENZA

ROGATION DAYS

Under the orchards, under
The tree strung vines, little blue
Figures are making hay, high
On the steep hillsides above
Palladio's drowsy villas
And Tiepolo's swirling walls.
On the highest field they are
Still cutting with swinging scythes;
Down below they are tossing
The long swathes of hay to cure
In the sun; further down they
Are cocking it, or carrying

It off in two-wheeled donkey carts.
The Venetian plain vanishes
In haze. The nearby Alps are
Indefinite blue smudges,
Capped with faint streaks of orange
Snow. Clouds of perfume roll up
The hillside in waves. All the birds
Sing. All the flowers bloom. Here
At a stone table like this,
On a little hill like this,
In a circle of cypress
And olive like this, the infinite
Visited Leopardi,
And ravished him and carried
Him off in the deep summer.
It would carry me off, too,
If I knew where I wanted
To go, or if I just wanted
To go nowhere at all.

ASCENSION NIGHT

I take a bath enveloped
In the essential odor of
Mediterranean civilization.
The ceiling high copper heater
At the foot of the tub
Is fired with sarments—
Prunings of vine and olive.
Down below the blossoming
Cherry trees full of nightingales
An electronic voice calls the trains
As they go through sleeping Vicenza
Bound for Paris, Belgrade, Munich.
Downstairs in the chapel,
The sisters are saying compline.
Next door in the bedroom,
My girls are all asleep.
The last penny rocket
Rises from the street fair.
Moonlight over the Alps
In a stormy sky.

Poems at Casa Paganelli, Campo San Zaccaria,

VENICE

MAY DAY

Once more it is early summer,
Like an opal, in Venice.
I listen to the monks sing
Vespers in San Giorgio Maggiore.
Ten years have gone by. I am
No longer alone. My little
Daughter and I sit hand in hand,
As the falling sunlight rises
Up Palladio's noble aisles
And shimmers in the incense.
The incense billows over
The altar. The *Magnificat*
Of May Day surges through the incense.
Six years ago, another May Day,
Mary played in a meadow stream,
And caught emerald green baby frogs.
Overhead then, dive bombers wrote
Monograms of death in the sky.
They are still there. Now they have
A new trick. At "He has put down
The mighty from their seat," one
Of them breaks the sound barrier
With a shuddering belch of hate,
One omnipresent sound in
The sky of Tiepolo.
The same shave jowled apes sit at
The same round mahogany tables,
Just across those pretty mountains.
They are pushing all this pretty
Planet, Venice, and Palladio,
And you and me, and the golden
Sun, nearer and nearer to
Total death. Nothing can stop them.
Soon it will be over. But
This music, and the incense,

And the solemn columned thought,
And the poem of a virgin,
And you and me, and Venice
In the May Day evening on the
Fiery waters, we have our own
Eternity, so fleeting that they
Can never touch it, or even
Know that it has passed them by.

ROSE COLORED GLASSES

Ten years, and it's still on the
Radio. *La Vie en rose*
Spills out of a dozen windows
Onto the canal. A woman
And her son in a vegetable
Barge sing it. A man polishing
The prow of his gondola
Sings it while his dog wags its tail.
Children playing hopscotch sing it.
Grimy half washed clothes hang overhead.
Garbage floats in the narrow canal.
More radios join in. Across
The canal, beyond the iron windows
Of the Women's Prison, a hundred
Pure voices of pickpockets
And prostitutes start to sing it.
It is just like being in church.
The next number is *Ciao, ciao, bambina*.

OBSERVATIONS
IN A CORNISH TEASHOP

How can they write or paint
In a country where it
Would be nicer to be
Fed intravenously?

WRITTEN TO MUSIC

EIGHT FOR ORNETTE'S MUSIC

if the pain is greater
than the difference
as the bird in the night
or the perfumes in the moon
oh witch of question
oh lips of submission
in the flesh of summer
the silver slipper
in the sleeping forest
if hope surpasses the question
by the mossy spring
in the noon of harvest
between the pillars of silk
in the luminous difference
oh tongue of music
oh teacher of splendor
if the meat of the heart
if the fluid of the wing
as love
if birth
or trust as
love as love

is it dreaming falling in
the tangling light
calls the light
the small sharp wafers
in the whirlpool
on white plume
floating
in the sky the blades
nibbling the breasts
new trembling
discover honey
kiss kiss

She didn't say where

nobody home
they all left
lipstick letters stockings
torn
a star
on the sooty pane
deep in the far off forest
initials and hearts entwined
nobody ever comes back
night planes
over village sky rockets
the most wonderful one
we ever had
darling
in the drawer
the chambermaid
found 1000
counterfeit
$10 bills

then the waning
moon in young leaves
do you think of the old wounds
it is like Mykenai
with those terrible
dead kings with gold foil
over their faces
no animal or vegetable
anywhere
another landscape
with some people in a boat
sewn with needles or with thread
birds with dry human voices

who issues certificates
to whom it may concern:
the bearer is alive
turn on the sky
take off your dress
saw down the tree
climb the mountain
kiss the lips
close the eyes
speak low
open
come

time turns like tables
the indifferent and blissful Spring
saves all souls and seeds and slaves asleep
dark Spring
in the dark whispering human will
words spoken by two kissing tongues
hissing union
Eve's snake
stars come on
two naked bodies tumble
through bodiless Christmas trees
blazing like bees and rosebuds
fire turns to falling powder
lips relax and smile and sleep
fire sweeps
the hearth of the blood
on far off red double stars
they probate their own tied wills

Blues

the sea will be deep
the eye will be deep
the last bell has been deep

the iceberg has been cold
the nail has been cold
the hungry whore was cold

the jungle was fierce
the tooth was fierce
the poor bum's woman is fierce

the plate of tripe is shallow
the omelette in the pan is shallow
shallow as the wisdom of the ages

the hawk in the zenith knows
the mole under the spade knows
the curly brain knows too

don't you forget it

Blues

grey as the arctic
grey as the sea
grey as the heart
grey as the bird in the tree

red as the sun
red as the robin
red as the heart
red as the axe in the tree

blue as the star
blue as the gull
blue as the heart
blue as the air in the tree

black as the tongue
black as the vulture
black as the heart
black as the hanged girl in the tree

TWO FOR BREW AND DICK

State and 32nd, Cold Morning Blues

A girl in a torn chemise
Weeps by a dirty window.
Jaws are punched in the street.

A cat is sick in the gutter.
Dogs bark up nightbound alleys.
There's nothing like the sorrow

Of the jukeboxes at dawn.
Dice girls going home.
Whores eating chop suey.

Pimps eat chile mac.
Drowsy flatfeet, ham and eggs.
Dawn of labor, dawn of life.

The awakening noises
Of the old sacrifices.
The snow blows down the bare street

Ahead of the first streetcar.
The lovers light cigarettes,
And part with burning eyes,

And go off in the daylight.

Married Blues

I didn't want it, you wanted it.
Now you've got it you don't like it.
You can't get out of it now.

Pork and beans, diapers to wash,
Too poor for the movies, too tired to love.
There's nothing we can do.

Hot stenographers on the subway.
The grocery boy's got a big one.
We can't do anything about it.

You're only young once.
You've got to go when your time comes.
That's how it is. Nobody can change it.

Guys in big cars whistle.
Freight trains moan in the night.
We can't get away with it.

That's the way life is.
Everybody's in the same fix.
It will never be any different.

AIR AND ANGELS

[Eric Satie: *Gymnopédie #1*]

Moonlight   now   on Malibu
The winter night   the few stars
Far away   millions   of miles
The sea   going on   and on
Forever   around   the earth
Far   and   far   as your lips   are near
Filled   with the same light   as your eyes
Darling   darling   darling
The future   is long gone by
And the past   will never happen
We have   only this
Our one forever
So small   so infinite
So brief   so vast
Immortal   as our hands that touch
Deathless   as the firelit wine we drink
Almighty   as this single kiss
That has no beginning
That will never
Never
End

AT LEAST THAT ABANDON

As I watch at the long window
Crowds of travelers hurry
Behind me, rainy darkness
Blows before me, and the great plane
Circles, taxis to the runway,
Waits, and then roars off into
The thick night. I follow it
As it rises through the clouds
And levels off under the stars.
Stars, darkness, a row of lights,

Moaning engines, thrumming wings,
A silver plane over a sea
Of starlit clouds and rain bound
Sea. What I am following
Is a rosy, glowing coal
Shaped like the body of a
Woman—rushing southward a
Meteor afire with the
Same fire that burns me unseen
Here on the whirling earth amongst
Bright, busy, incurious
Faces of hundreds of people
Who pass me, unaware of
The blazing astrophysics
Of the end of a weekend.

AN EASY SONG

It's rained every day since you
Went away. I've been lonely.
Lonely, empty, tenderness—
Longing to kiss the corners
Of your mouth as you smile
Your special, inward, sensual,
And ironic smile I love
Because I know it means you
Are content—*content* in French—
A special, inward, sensual,
And ironic state of bliss.
Tu es contente, ma chèrie?
I am, even if lonely,
Because I can call to mind
Your body in a warm room,
In the rainy winter night,
A rose on the hearth of winter,
A rose cloud standing naked,
In the perfume of your flesh.
Moi aussi, je suis content.

COMING

You are driving to the airport
Along the glittering highway
Through the warm night,
Humming to yourself.
The yellow rose buds that stood
On the commode faded and fell
Two days ago. Last night the
Petals dropped from the tulips
On the dresser. The signs of
Your presence are leaving the
House one by one. Being without
You was almost more than I
Could bear. Now the work is squared
Away. All the arrangements
Have been made. All the delays
Are past and I am thirty
Thousand feet in the air over
A dark lustrous sea, under
A low half moon that makes the wings
Gleam like fish under water—
Rushing south four hundred miles
Down the California coast
To your curving lips and your
Ivory thighs.

PACIFIC BEACH

This is the sea called peaceful,
And tonight it is quiet
As sleeping flesh under
The October waning moon.
Late night, not a moving car
On all the moonlit Coast Highway.
No sound but the offshore bells
And the long, recurrent hiss
Of windless surf. "Sophocles
Long ago heard it by the
Aegean." I drive eighty
Miles an hour through the still,

Moonfilled air. The surf withdraws,
Returns, and brings into my
Mind the turgid ebb and flow
Of human loyalty—
The myriad ruined voices
That have said, "Ah, love, let us
Be true to one another."
The moon lured voyagers sleep
In all the voiceless city.
Far out on the horizon
The lights of the albacore
Fleet gleam like a golden town
In another country.

MAROON BELLS

How can I love you more than
The silver whistle of the
Coney in the rocks loves you?
How can I love you better
Than the blue of the bluebells
By the waterfall loves you?
Eater of moonlight, drinker
Of brightness, feet of jewels
On the mountain, velvet feet
In the meadow grass, darkness
Braided with wild roses, wild
Mare of all the horizons . . . .
A far away tongue speaks in
The time that fills me like a
Tongue in a bell falling
Out of all the towers of space.
Eyes wide, nostrils distended,
We drown in secret happy
Oceans we trade in broad daylight.
O my girl, mistress of all
Illuminations and all
Commonplaces, I love you
Like the air and the water
And the earth and the fire and
The light love you and love you.

ASPEN MEADOWS

Look. Listen. They are lighting
The moon. Be still. I don't want
To hear again that wistful
Kyriale of husbands and lovers.
Stop questioning me
About my women. You are
Not a schoolgirl nor I a
Lecturing paleobotanist.
It's enough that the green glow
Runs through the down on your arms
Like a grass fire and your eyes
Are fogs of the same endless light.
Let the folds and divisions
Of your anatomy envelop
All horizons. O my sweet
Topology and delusion,
You may be arrogant and feral
But no clock can measure
How long ago you fell asleep
In my arms in the midst of
Sliding doors, parting curtains,
Electric fishes and candy lotuses
And the warm wet moonlight.

LIKE QUEEN CHRISTINA

Orange and blue and then grey
The frosty twilight comes down
Through the thin trees. The fresh snow
Holds the light longer than the sky.
Skaters on the pond vanish
In dusk, but their voices stay,
Calling and laughing, and birds
Twitter and cry in the reeds.
Indoors as night fills the white rooms,
You stand in the candle light
Laughing like a splendid jewel.

INDEX OF TITLES AND FIRST LINES

Poem titles are printed in *italic* type.

343